RESEARCHING LIFE STORIES
AND
FAMILY HISTORIES

INTRODUCING QUALITATIVE METHODS provides a series of volumes which introduce qualitative research to the student and beginning researcher. The approach is interdisciplinary and international. A distinctive feature of these volumes is the helpful student exercises.

One stream of the series provides texts on the key methodologies used in qualitative research. The other stream contains books on qualitative research for different disciplines or occupations. Both streams cover the basic literature in a clear and accessible style, but also cover the 'cutting edge' issues in the area.

SERIES EDITOR
David Silverman (Goldsmiths College)

EDITORIAL BOARD
Michael Bloor (University of Wales, Cardiff)
Barbara Czarniawska-Joerges (University of Gothenburg)
Norman Denzin (University of Illinois, Champagne)
Barry Glassner (University of Southern California)
Jaber Gubrium (University of Florida, Gainesville)
Anne Murcott (South Bank University)
Jonathan Potter (Loughborough University)

TITLES IN SERIES
Doing Conversational Analysis: A Practical Guide
Paul ten Have

Using Foucault's Methods
Gavin Kendall and Gary Wickham

The Quality of Qualitative Evaluation
Clive Seal

Qualitative Evaluation
Ian Shaw

Researching Life Stories and Family Histories
Robert L. Miller

RESEARCHING LIFE STORIES
AND
FAMILY HISTORIES

Robert L. Miller

SAGE Publications
London • Thousand Oaks • New Delhi

ISBN 0-7619-6091-0 (hbk)
ISBN 0-7619-6092-9 (pbk)
© Robert L. Miller 2000
First published 2000

SAGE Publications Ltd
1 Oliver's Yard,
55 City Road
London EC1Y 1SP

SAGE Publications Inc
2455 Teller Road
Thousand Oaks,
California 91320

SAGE Publications India Pvt Ltd
B–42 Panchsheel Enclave
PO Box 4109
New Delhi 110 017

British Library Cataloguing in Publication data
A catalogue record for this book is available from the British Library

Printed digitally and bound in Great Britain by
Lightning Source UK Ltd., Milton Keynes, Bedfordshire

Contents

Preface

Changes in the conduct of social science often have been dramatic. The application of quantitative statistical techniques to social data during the period following the Second World War was a revolution of sorts, bringing the social sciences much more to the centre and contributing immeasurably to their prestige and standing relative to the natural sciences. Ironically, just when this paradigm began to attain its zenith through the availability of computer-aided statistical modelling, the complacency of 1950s functionalist social science was rocked by the political upheavals of the late 1960s which led directly to the radical 'critical' analyses of social structure, the feminist challenge to 'malestream' social science and to the (re)discovery of paradigms of qualitative social research. In their turn, the ideological sureties of critical theories, original 'second wave' feminism and accepted modes of qualitative research each have had their foundations undermined by the relativistic questioning of postmodernism. These shifts have been highly visible.

But changes need neither to be highly visible nor dramatic in order to be significant. The emergence of what now can be termed the biographical perspective follows this latter, quieter, pattern. In the West, qualitative researchers seeking to elicit in-depth information found themselves being led by their research subjects away from directed reports toward more discursive but informative narrative accounts of careers and life stories (Chase, 1995). Researchers in a variety of substantive areas who were seeking means of moving away from an atomistic focus on the present situation of single individuals were led to adopt perspectives that covered whole lives (for example, the life course research of Martin Kohli) or whole families across several generations (for example, the multi-generational family history charts of Bertaux 1995 or Andorka 1997).

Eastern Europe has had a strong popular tradition of life histories that has spanned the century. In particular during the decades after the Second World War an Orwellian situation existed in eastern European societies in which face-to-face communication could be a more reliable source of social and historical information than tightly controlled official sources, which led to a readiness to accept orally generated knowledge there.

These trends began to accelerate at the end of the 1960s. The result is that for upwards of a quarter of a century the use of biographical methods, including the taking of family histories, has been a lively and developing area of sociology (Simeoni and Diani 1995; Bertaux and Kohli 1984). The full programme of activities of the International Sociolgical Association's Biography and Society Research Committee is one of the clearest indicators of the area's health. Comparative research also takes place at the continental level through bodies such as the Biographical Perspectives on European Societies Research Network and at the national level through groups such as the Biographical Research Section of the German Sociological Association and the British Sociological Association's Auto/Biography Working Group. The rate of publication of monographs and edited book series (for example, Passerini 1992) is healthy and there is a small but growing number of texts concerned with the area. Biographical and family history research has now been applied to numerous substantive areas, employing a variety of theoretical viewpoints.

As stated above, the biographical perspective is an emergent perspective coalescing out of research activity in a number of disciplines that has been taking place in a variety of countries both in Europe and North America. To date, there has not been a single text that synthesizes the streams of biographical research that have developed independently. This book is an attempt to carry out this task. It will take the view that three differing approaches can be identified within the biographical perspective. These approaches can be labelled as the *realist* approach, the *neo-positivist* approach, and the *narrative* approach. While research practitioners may be eclectic in the techniques they adopt, pragmatically using insights from several or all three of these approaches, each has its own unique core of insight which it brings to the biographical perspective. The realist approach subscribes to grounded theory techniques of research and is based fundamentally in processes of inducing concepts from empirical data. The neo-positivist approach emphasizes the empirical testing of pre-existing conceptual frameworks. The narrative approach centres upon the process of constructing a view of reality that is carried out jointly by the researcher and the interviewee.

Overview of the book

Chapter 1   Introduction The book begins by explaining the broad expanse of the techniques of life histories and family histories, how these two techniques are complementary and how they differ from the 'cross-sectional' approach implicit in much social science research. An account is given of the sporadic development and use in the social sciences of life and family histories. Three basic perspectives on the life and family history methods – the 'realist', the 'cultural' and the 'narrative' – are introduced. Their current development and applications in an international context are surveyed.

Chapter 2   The Historical Context The collection of life histories brings questions of time to the fore that are obscured or neglected by more conventional research. The conceptualization of time and how one uses it in analysis has been central to biographical research. 'Time effects' can be placed into five categories: ageing; generations; cohorts; historical trends; and period effects. Age is a structural variable of central importance and of significance equal to that of other structural variables such as gender, social class and racial or ethnic group. The term 'generation' has multiple meanings and needs to be clarified into (i) generations in the sense of parent/children family generations and (ii) periods of significant social experience – cohort generations. Correctly identifying true historical trends is central to understanding social change. Period effects raise important issues of the interplay of historical events and social change and also pose questions of reliability.

Chapter 3   Collecting and Organizing Family Histories   Even though most people live most of their lives in families, mainstream social research works under the illusion that humans are isolated individuals anchored only within large aggregate collectivities. The collection of family histories promotes a view in which the family, rather than the individual, becomes the central unit of analysis. Families are important avenues for the transmission of capital – material, social and cultural. Important topics of social research, such as migration and social mobility, appear different when one realizes that mobility is not scattered randomly in a population but rather often clusters in families. The family history approach leads one to concentrate upon questions such as: family strategies; the unequal allocation of resources within families; the control and passing on of wealth and status; questions of patriarchy and matriarchy and authority; the familial 'micro' as a reflection of the societal 'macro'; 'skeletons in family closets'; how missing or unobtainable information provides clues for analysis; contradictory descriptions of the same family events.

In recent years the collection of family histories has undergone extensive development. In order to give students practical experience of these developments, this chapter adopts a different format from the conceptual discussions of its predecessors and is based upon a series of practical exercises. The first exercise is the construction of a 'rectangular' family history chart across three generations. In the second exercise, quantitative information is extracted from the family history grid and placed into a series of tables. Analysis of the grid and tables reveals phenomena such as changes in fertility, levels of education, occupational mobility, and migration across the generations. In a third exercise (which may be done in combination with the interviewing exercise of Chapter 4), students conduct two interviews with members of the same family of different genders from different generations. The interviews are centred around a single substantive topic, such as social mobility within the family, and are intended to highlight how different locations within the social structure of the same family can lead to varying perspectives on the same phenomena.

Chapter 4   Collecting Life Histories   This chapter discusses issues pertaining to the collection of biographies with special attention paid to interviewing techniques and the long time perspective implicit within the life history. Topics covered include: selecting and approaching respondents for interview; the 'interview contract' with a respondent; semi-structured and unstructured interviewing; note-taking; reacting to notes when framing subsequent interviews; doing a series of interviews with a single respondent. It is naïve to believe that the experience of giving a life history is always positive – respondents giving life histories can find themselves reliving painful episodes in their past or re-evaluating their lives; considerations such as these raise ethical issues which are discussed in the chapter.

The three approaches to biographical research presented in the book – the Realist, the neo-Positivist, and the Narrative – each imply different modes of interviewing. In order to illustrate the differences between these modes, a series of interviews employing the contrasting techniques were carried out with one individual. The person chosen for this in-depth treatment was 'William', a middle-aged married professional living in Northern Ireland. Extracts from his interviews provide the core illustrative material for this chapter and the following chapter on approaches to analysis. While these extracts will give many details about William, a brief 'potted biography' of his life will be given here.

William is a Protestant whose family has been located in Ulster for generations. His father was a doctor and his mother was a housewife. William is the eldest of his siblings, was born in the early 1950s and grew up in a provincial market town in Northern Ireland. His secondary education was as a boarder in a select grammar school and he subsequently attended the Queen's University of Belfast, where he obtained a professional qualification. After qualifying, he worked for more than ten years in different public-sector jobs and then moved into private practice. William married in his mid-30s and has one son. He has been heavily involved in sports throughout his life, first as a competitor and later as the organizer of many sporting events and as a committee officer for a large sports club. As well as his sporting commitments, he also maintains a full calendar of public-service activities.

This chapter concludes with an exercise on the collection of a life history/life story from a middle-aged or elderly individual.

Students carry out two interviews – an initial unfocused interview which is then followed up with a second interview centred on a substantive topic of their choice that would be relevant to a whole lifetime (for example, 'a working life', 'building a family'). The interviews are only loosely structured in order to allow maximum opportunity for methodological issues associated with the narrative approach to arise.

Chapter 5   Analysing Life Histories   This chapter brings to the fore methodological issues raised by the three approaches to biographical research. Modes of data collection for both biographies and family histories have seen much advancement and standardization in recent years but agreed methods of analysis still await development. The realist approach sees both life stories and family histories as means of collecting factual empirical material. The goal of analysis is the generation of concepts through induction and grounded theory techniques. As such, the realist approach is concerned with issues of factual reliability and views 'saturation' (multiple cases revealing the same patterns) as a solution and may depict the life or family history as a 'microcosm' that reflects (some aspects of) 'the macrocosm'. In the neo-positivist approach, there is an interplay between the 'actor' and 'structure'. The goal of analysis is the validation of pre-existing theory through the deductive evaluation of concepts against empirical information. In contrast to the other approaches, the narrative approach is based fundamentally in the ongoing development of the respondent's viewpoint. Here, questions of fact take second place to understanding an individual's unique and changing perspective as it is mediated by social context, including the context of the life history interview itself.

Chapter 6   Conclusion   The final chapter summarizes the features of the three approaches to biographical research and speculates about the genesis of an overarching biographical perspective. In order to construct their biography, the individual must take account of their past history and its working through the present to an anticipated future. The 'account taking' includes an estimation of preceding social structures, their future evolution and the person's own placement in them. This 'embeddedness' in time and structure is necessary for an individual's own sense of autobiography. Biographical analysis requires an analogous 'embeddedness'. The adoption of a biographical perspective in social research implies transcending barriers of self/society and past/present/future. This transcendent nature of biographical research opens prospects for a significant advance in sociological conceptualization.

1

Introduction

CONTENTS

'Tell us the story of your life.'

This apparently simple request has led to a quiet revolution in social science practice. For it even to be seen as a legitimate query required a shift in paradigmatic viewpoints about the nature of the social scientific enterprise. How to elicit a comprehensive response to this request has required the development of new techniques of interviewing. The answers that this request can elicit lead to profound methodological deliberations about the nature of social reality and the kind of knowing that is possible for a sociological researcher.

Since the early 1970s a unique perspective has been (re)-emerging in the social sciences. Variously termed the life history or life story approach, life course research, the (auto)biographical perspective or the narrative approach, this view of social research activity has its roots in techniques of sociological practice that were current during the period between the two

World Wars. Working independently of each other, practitioners in the various social science disciplines – anthropology, sociology, psychology, social policy, political science – located in North America and western and eastern Europe began to revive a truly sociological perspective that emphasizes the placement of individuals within an ongoing and evolving social structure. This viewpoint will here be termed the biographical perspective.

Despite its multifarious origins, the emergent biographical perspective now has coalesced to the extent that some common features can be identified. Rather than limiting itself to the slice of an individual's situation located at the present, the focus of interest is upon people's complete lives or, at the very least, upon a significant portion of people's lives. This broadening of focus has profound implications for sociological practice. To begin with, questions of time come to the fore. While normally the primary locus of information is the present, in biographical research the past and people's experience of the past takes on a much more central significance than usual. Additionally, present activity can be seen as formed as much by the anticipation of the future as it is by the experience of the past. Rigour is required in the use of time-related concepts such as the meaning of generations, the perception of true historical change and the identification of age cohorts. In terms of method, profound and complex issues concerning the reliability of recall and the validity of using present-day information to study the past are raised.

Furthermore, the maintenance of the fiction of the atomized individual becomes untenable with adoption of a biographical perspective. Lives are lived within social networks from early socialization on. People grow up in families, move into and through educational systems and labour markets, become subject to the regimes of health institutions and the like.

The importance of the family, both the family of origin and the later family that a person may establish, can be central to understanding the biographies of individuals. This centrality, and the overlap in methodological issues that apply to biographical research and the study of family histories, will lead this book to concentrate upon family history research as well as the biographical perspective.

While the use of biographical methods is an active and

rapidly developing area of research, what is not so clear, however, are the methodological parameters that define this area. Is there a 'biographical perspective' on sociological endeavour that unifies those subscribing to it through the provision of a common methodological framework? Alternatively, is biographical and family history research a broad topic area which can harbour a number of different, perhaps contradictory, approaches?

The question of which view is more correct has significant implications for the development of biographical and family history research. If the former unifying view holds, the fundamental issues are those of syncretism – how to establish the essential traits of an emerging 'biographical perspective', how to merge different approaches and reconcile apparent divergences and, if one is doctrinal, how to eliminate heresies. If the latter is the case, the need to clarify approaches to biographical research remains, only with implications that are simultaneously more centripetal and centrifugal. If the only unifying trait of biographical methods is the broad arena in which the research takes place, the need to resolve contradictions between approaches is less pressing. In fact, there can be different ways of carrying out biographical research whose only common feature happens to be that the 'data' is a biography or life history. At the same time, however, if coincidence of research arena *is* the only feature that biographical researchers have in common, the implications are divisive. If there are several unique ways of carrying out biographical research, the need to interact with those subscribing to different approaches may not be vital and researchers employing varying biographical techniques could afford to be indifferent to each other.

Origins

The origins of biographical and family history approaches can provide insight into the question of whether a unitary or multiple viewpoint determines the way biographical research should be practiced at the beginning of a new millenium. Biographies as a literary genre run back at least as far as Augustine. Their development can be seen as a result of the

new consciousness of the Enlightenment in which the importance of the individual as an actor independent of family or
position was asserted (cf. Plummer 1983: 8–10; Kohli 1986a: 94;
Chanfrault-Duchet 1995: 209–10). The writing of biographies,
accounts of the lives of persons who have a significant impact
upon public events, and the keeping of personal diaries and
their public versions, autobiographies, became meaningful. The
first social scientific concern with biographical perspective,
however, did not develop until nineteenth-century Germany:

> The first author to turn life history into an object to be theorized by
> the human sciences was Dilthey (1833–1911), who viewed 'life story
> as a whole, an object complete unto itself'. To analyse the object and
> grasp the significance of life experience in its singularity, Dilthey
> developed the 'comprehensive method', based on empathy, later to
> be reconsidered and refined by Weber. And yet, despite several
> attempts at laying out the foundations for a sociological biograph-
> ical approach, Dilthey's ideas have remained attached to the literary
> pole of the human sciences. (Chanfrault-Duchet 1995: 210; see also
> Kohli, 1986a: 95–6)

Dilthey's attempts to bring a biographical perspective to the
social sciences, however, may not have been completely in vain.
It is likely that Dilthey's concern with 'life and lived experience'
was one of the European influences that affected Robert Park of
the first Department of Sociology in the United States at the
University of Chicago (Plummer 1983: 52).

The University of Chicago and the humanistic pragmatic
version of sociology known as 'the Chicago School' was the
single most significant variety of sociology in the United States
from the beginning of the twentieth century until well into
the period between the two World Wars. The Department of
Sociology at the University of Chicago was the first in the
United States and it was *the* place for sociology in America until
well into the 1930s (Madge 1962). The life history method was
central to the Chicago School. The first sociological use of the
technique took place immediately prior to the First World War
with the 300-page life story of Wladek Wisznienski, a Polish
immigrant to America, which formed a central part of *The Polish
Peasant in Europe and America* study of W.I. Thomas and Florian
Znaniecki. During the 1920s and 1930s, this and other life

histories carried out by the Chicago School (most notably C.R. Shaw's *The Jack Roller* (1966), a life history of a juvenile delin- quent) were one of *the* two main methods of sociological research in the United States (the other was the use of quantitat- ive data and statistical analyses). During the period between the World Wars in the United States, the main methodological debate was between the life history or 'case study' method and the 'statistical' method.

Life histories as they were practiced by the Chicago School displayed features that still distinguish the biographical per- spective. The subjects from which the histories were elicited were common people, only notable in that they sometimes may be associated with somewhat illicit or 'unrespectable' activity. Advocacy, or at least sympathy, with their position was implicit. 'The classic natural-history interactionist approach to life stories. . . . gave delinquents, prostitutes, alcoholics, drug addicts and immigrants traits, personalities, personality flaws and chances to tell their stories. It transformed subjects into sociologies' (Denzin 1995: 120). The viewpoint of the method was holistic, with the ideal being a detailed and as complete collection of information as possible. The method was distinctly qualitative and, while not necessarily anti-positivistic, certainly did not attach primacy to aggregate data. Quotation from Thomas and Znaniecki is illustrative:

> Whether we draw our materials for sociological analysis from detailed life records of concrete individuals or from the observation of mass phenomena, the problems of sociological analysis are the same. We are safe in saying that personal life records, as complete as possible, constitute the *perfect* type of sociological material and that if social science has to use other material at all it is only because of the practical difficulty of obtaining at the moment a sufficient number of such records to cover the totality of sociological prob- lems, and of the enormous amount of work demanded for an adequate analysis of all the personal material necessary to charac- terize the life of a social group. If we are forced to use mass phenomena as material, or any kind of happenings taken without regard to the life histories of the individuals who participate in them, it is a defect, not an advantage, of our present sociological method. (Thomas and Znaniecki 1958: 1823–4)

Finally, the Chicago variant of the life history method was an action perspective in that it took account of both the influences of social structure in providing opportunities or constraints for the actor along with the actor's own ability to perceive these opportunities/constraints subjectively and react to them creatively.

The life history method employed in Chicago had connections with Europe through the collection of *pamietniki* – written autobiographies or memoirs usually solicited through competitions run by newspapers (Chalasinski 1991). Znaniecki, one of the authors of *The Polish Peasant in Europe and America*, organized the first *pamietniki* competition in Poland in 1921 (Bertaux 1981: 3).

By the 1930s the life history method was being employed on both sides of the Atlantic; in North America as a central part of the 'Golden Age' of the Chicago School of sociology and in Europe in the form of the important *pamietniki* movement. This situation, however, was to prove a false dawn for the biographical perspective. The rise of the research paradigm of quantitative survey research and data analysis totally eclipsed the life history method, so that by the immediate post-World War II period it had gone (Plummer 1983).[1] The reasons for this eclipse are not completely clear. The academic literature of the *pamietniki* movement had not been translated and, while it remained active as a Polish tradition, it had nil international impact (Bertaux and Kohli 1984) – a situation exacerbated by the isolation of eastern European sociology from the West during the period of the Cold War. In the West and particularly in North America, the overwhelming dominance of quantitative methods of research meant that life history techniques faded along with the rest of the qualitative paradigm.

While proponents of the current streams of biographical research have traced their conceptual lineage back to these pre-World War II studies, the present-day interest in biography has its true origins as part of the 'qualitative backlash' against the dominance of the quantitative approach. C. Wright Mills' *The Sociological Imagination*, first published in 1959, is a seminal text for the resurgence of the biographical perspective. In it, Mills echoed Thomas and Znaniecki and took the position that, 'Social science deals with problems of biography, of history, and of their intersections within social structures. . . . these three –

biography, history, society – are the coordinate points of the proper study of man' (Mills 1959: 159). A new generation entered academia in the 1960s. It was sparked by the political and cultural turmoil of the decade – the rise of the counter-culture, civil rights movements in the United States and Northern Ireland, the anti-Vietnam War movement in the United States and the events of 1968 in Europe. Many of these students turned to sociology as an aid to interpreting the events in which they found themselves embroiled. What they found, particularly in the English-speaking world, was a sociology woefully incapable of interpreting the social reality of the 1960s. Mainstream sociology mired in Parsonian functionalism emphasized equilibrium as the norm and was incapable of explaining change. Mills' *Sociological Imagination* was one of the few key texts in the sociological canon that spoke directly to the intellectual needs of the day. While *Sociological Imagination* is not a text directly concerned with the application of the biographical perspective, the interplay between personal biography, history, and society is at its core. This seminal text was a core influence upon a generation of sociological students and was instrumental in laying the groundwork for the resurgence of biographical methods that began to take place towards the beginning of the next decade. Under the auspices of Daniel Bertaux, a working group on the life history method with its members drawn from a variety of countries began to meet in the late 1970s. This group subsequently developed into the International Sociology Association's Research Committee 38, 'Biography and Society' – with almost 500 members currently one of the most active of the ISA Research Committees.[2]

The features of the current biographical approach share much in common with the general impetus behind the 'qualitative backlash' of the early 1970s of which it was a part. The positivistic assumptions of quantitative analysis were criticized – in particular the use of statistical techniques to test hypotheses as a means of advancing abstract theory. Qualitative methods have more 'breadth'; they are not limited to only a small number of variables in their analyses. Qualitative techniques are not as dependent upon the financial resources necessary in order to carry out a large-scale probability survey.[3] The rich description possible with qualitative techniques allow for the depiction of process – ongoing or developing phenomena.

These features – general to all qualitative techniques – had substantive effects. Firstly, new and interesting topic areas could be opened up. Data collection with qualitative methods could be much more exploratory and less constrained by pre-determined protocols. If researchers were willing to invest the time and gamble their own careers, mundane considerations such as obtaining a grant or access to a mainframe computer were less of a factor. Secondly, being less dependent upon vetted funding, the topics covered by qualitative methods could be more controversial. Biographical methods had a strong humanist impetus in that they provided a means of conducting research that gave voice to the (to use current terminology) 'socially excluded' (Bertaux 1996). The work of Oscar Lewis (*La Vida, The Children of Sanchez*) was particularly influential (Bertaux and Kohli 1984). Lewis says: 'One of the major objectives of my recent work has been to give a voice to people who are rarely heard and to provide readers with an inside view of a style of life which is common in many of the deprived and marginal groups of our society' (Lewis 1970: xiv). Through biographical and other qualitative research techniques, faceless 'cases' could attain[4] an identity that a quantitative analysis must deny them.

It was the features of breadth and process that particularly distinguished biographical and family history methods from other qualitative techniques. The holistic approach of the biography and the family history leads to broader depictions of individuals' identities both across time and in the social networks that support them (Bertaux 1995). Amongst types of qualitative research, the information obtained through biographical methods or family histories contrasted most extremely with quantitative data. The breadth of coverage of a biography that could span all aspects of an individual's lifetime over almost a century or of a family history that could cover dozens or more people held together by a complex network of social relations was far removed from a variable-based quantitative dataset based upon a probability sample of individuals taken at a single cross-section of historical time and place. 'The perspective (or point of view) of life history research . . . is the totality of the biographical experience. . . . As such more than almost any other method it allows one to grasp a sense of the totality of a life. As Bogdan says [at the beginning of *The Autobiography of Jane Fry'* 1974: 4]:

> The autobiography is unique in allowing us to view an individual in the context of his [sic] whole life, from birth to the point at which we encounter him. Because of this it can lead us to a fuller understanding of the stages and critical periods in the processes of his development. It enable us to look at subjects as if they have a past with successes as well as failures, and a future with hopes and fears. It also allows us to see an individual in relation to the history of his time, and how he is influenced by the various religious, social, psychological and economic currents present in his world. It permits us to view the intersection of the life history of men with the history of their society, thereby enabling us to understand better the choices, contingencies and options open to the individual.[5] (In Plummer 1983: 69)

As the above quote implies, *process* also distinguishes the biographical perspective from other qualitative approaches. Becker's observations on the advantages of the life history in his introduction to *The Jack Roller* are singularly appropriate:

> The life history, more than any other technique except perhaps participant observation, can give meaning to the overworked notion of *process*. Sociologists like to speak of 'ongoing processes' and the like but their methods usually prevent them from seeing the processes they talk about so glibly. (Becker 1970: 424–5)

Furthermore, within the biographical perspective, 'process' has a particular double-edged meaning. When a person's lifetime is viewed as a whole, the idea of their 'history' can be apprehended at two levels. First, the individual has their own history of personal development and change as they 'process' along their life course. Second, a considerable amount of time passes as they move along their life course. In this respect, historical events and social change at the societal level impinge upon the individual's own unique life history.

Hence, early biographical and family history research has some features in common with other qualitative techniques that set it apart from the quantitative paradigm – a general antipathy towards and suspicion of quantitative approaches remains, controversial/political topics are more possible due to a comparative independence from funding support requirements and qualitative research exhibits a humanist/inclusive impetus generally. As well, however, the holistic aspects of biographies and family histories, by emphasizing the individual as a unique entity located in a complex network of social relationships that change and evolve over historical time, distinguish the biographical approach from other qualitative techniques.[6]

Three approaches

The newfound popularity of the biographical perspective has led to a resurgence of research work and conceptual development on both sides of the Atlantic and in western and eastern Europe. The original insights of the biographical perspective – a commitment to a holistic approach which emphasizes breadth of content, an interest in questions of process and the interplay between personal and public history have been retained. At the same time, the perspective has developed – technological innovations such as the introduction of computer programs for the organization and analysis of qualitative data or even the availability of cheap and reliable cassette tape recorders have produced a geometric increase in the sheer amount of information that can be collected and processed by qualitative researchers. Distinct and new methodological approaches to the collection and analysis of biographical information have evolved. These methodological approaches are rarely (if ever) applied in their pure forms but rather in combination with each other. The manner of their combination has profound implication for the course of research adopted. Turning to the present-day use of biographical and family history methods, it will be the contention of this book that three basic approaches to the biographical perspective can be identified: a **realist** approach; a **neo-positivist** approach; and a **narrative** approach. The explication of these approaches and their use in the collection and analysis of biographical material will form the core of this book.

Before proceeding to explore the features of each of these approaches to biography and family history, two caveats need to be advanced. The first is that the initial depiction of these approaches will be made in an ideal-typical format in order to establish a 'pure' baseline for subsequent discussion. Real researchers operate across the borders of the approaches and, while they may be based primarily within one approach, they will be aware of the arguments and virtues that constitute the strengths of the other schools and will utilise features of the other approaches in a pragmatic manner. Indeed, an important goal of the book is to attempt to clarify confusions caused by the operational overlap of the approaches. Secondly, the labels used here are heuristic devices. There is a danger that any label which is applied may have unintended resonances, particularly in an international context.[7] Trying to avoid prejudging the features of the approaches by their labels and remembering that one is seeking to identify essentials, let us conduct a preliminary examination of each approach in turn.

Realist

The core of the realist approach is induction. Information collected through taking life or family histories is used to construct general principles concerning social phenomena. The collection of information should be as uncontaminated by prior suppositions or preconceptions as possible. Hence, non-directive modes of interviewing or soliciting information are indicated. The realist approach holds that the viewpoints of actors do represent an aspect of an objective reality – albeit these viewpoints may be partially misconstrued at the level of single individuals. An important principle of the inductive process is that of 'saturation' – multiple cases should be collected and should reveal the same patterns if they are to be accepted as a solution for generalization. Factual reliability is important for this approach.

While not all proponents of the realist approach would label themselves as such, links with grounded theory are clear (for example, Bertaux 1995). The realist approach implies collecting information from a cross-section of individuals with the criteria for selection corresponding to those of theoretical sampling. A sufficient number of cases is important, but as a means of obtaining a broad and varied basis upon which to generalize rather than for the purpose of generating a statistically representative probability sample.

Neo-positivist

This approach has the closest affinity with 'classical' sociology. The core of the neo-positivist approach is deduction. Pre-existing networks of concepts are used to make theoretically based predictions concerning people's experienced lives. The collection of information centres upon areas of theoretical concern and the mode is one of testing hypothetical predictions against observed or reported phenomena. Hence, focused modes of data collection or interviewing with semi-structured schedules are used. In common with the realist, the neo-positivist approach also posits the existence of an objective reality and holds that the perspectives of actors do represent aspects of that reality. Here, the hermeneutic interplay between the subjective perceptions of the actor and an objective social structure would be emphasized. The actor's perceptions will be a subjective view, a mediation between perception and structure. These subjective perceptions will be malleable further due to changes in structure and to the passage of time as the effects of past structural influences recede and alter in the individual's own recollections. Silverman, Gubrium and Holstein's question of 'Why behaviour takes the form it does' is relevant here (Silverman and Gubrium 1994; Holstein and Gubrium 1995). Issues of conceptual validity are important for this approach.

Narrative

The narrative approach bases itself fundamentally upon the ongoing development of the respondent's viewpoint during the telling of a life or family 'story'. Understanding the individual's unique and changing perspective as it is mediated by *context* takes precedence over questions of fact. In the narrative perspective, 'context' includes both positioning in social structure and time and, just as important, the social context of the interview itself. The interplay between the interview partnership of interviewee and interviewer is at the core of this approach. The two together are collaborators, composing and constructing a story the teller can be pleased with. As collaborator in an open-ended process, the researcher-guide is never really in control of the story actually told' (Atkinson 1998: 9). The narrative approach can be labelled 'postmodern', in that reality is seen to be situational and fluid – jointly constructed by the interview partnership during the conduct of the interview. The personal

Table 1   *Three approaches to biographical and family history research*

Realist	Neo-positivist	Narrative
Inductive	Deductive	Fluid nature of individual's standpoint actively constructed as an ongoing (situational) project
Grounded theory based upon factual empirical material	Theory testing through factual empirical material	
Reality arises from the respondents' perspectives	Focused interviews	Questions of fact take second place to understanding the individual's unique and changing perception
	The most hermeneutic – actor's subjective perspective as affected by social structure – the interplay between actor and structure	
Unfocused interviews		
Serendipity		
Saturation (multiple interviews with multiple respondents eventually reaching a point where little new is revealed by additional interviews)		Life or family stories
	Life or family history as a 'microcosm' of a 'macrocosm'	Reality structured by interplay between interviewee and interviewer in terms of representations (semiotics)
	Validity is important	
Life or family history as a 'microcosm' of a 'macrocosm'	The 'Why?' question (for example, why interaction proceeds as it does)	'Postmodern', 'chaotic', ethnomethodological
Reliability is important		Present is a lens through which past and future are seen
		Interplay between interviewee and interviewer as a 'microcosm' of a 'macrocosm'
		The 'How?' question (for example, how is context constituted?)

characteristics of the interviewer can constitute one of the main stimuli to the interviewee and there is not a blanket prohibition against the interviewer either reacting openly to the statements of the interviewee and/or revealing personal details of their own. In fact, the ethnomethodological question of 'How the interview context is constituted' (Silverman and Gubrium, 1994; Holstein and Gubrium, 1995) is central to the narrative approach. How the interview partnership generates the context and flow of the interview is used to provide insight into social life. The only real structure that is being explicated directly is that which pertains to the interview partnership at the place and time of the interview. In 'normal' life actors generate their ongoing perceptions of their social environments through inter-action with others and with their structural contexts – and the interview situation is seen as no more than a special instance of the general. The interplay of reactions between the interviewee and interviewer – the tensions, negotiations, agreements, accom-modations, and so on – provides insight into the only available social reality, the one that is ongoing at that time. Information about structure and process is obtained, but it is of a special nature – direct information about structure and process is only revealed in the relative statuses and interactions between the interview partners themselves. Information about any wider context is indirect, mediated through the perceptions generated during the course of interview interaction. While the narrative approach is tightly located in the present moment, remem-brances of the past and anticipations of the future are recon-structed continuously through the lens of the present (Kohli, 1981).

Overlaps

The three approaches delineated above can overlap consider-ably in practice. Researchers using biographical or family his-tory methods may choose not to place themselves formally within a single camp (and of course they are not under any compulsion even to recognize the division into the three ap-proaches I have put forward here). Furthermore, researchers are pragmatists and tend to select their research procedures on the basis of their utility for the task at hand rather than to reject them on the grounds of methodological purity (Davis 1997: 3).

The core of the realist approach is the use of inductive, grounded theory strategies in order to work from empirical observations to the generation of concepts. For no reason other than their social science training, however, Realists cannot maintain a fiction of ignoring all theorizing that has preceded them. Grounded theory procedures have never mandated that the researcher must rediscover the conceptual wheel and ignore all work that has preceded them (Corbin and Strauss 1990: 11). The choice of a research topic, pre-existing concepts and the current issues of academic debate will mould even the most non-directive set of interview prompts. The analyst will be a trained social scientist. The processes of selection and categorization that lead to the development of concepts do not take place in an intellectual vacuum and will be governed to some extent by at least oblique reference to existing theory.

Similarly, while a neo-Positivist may operate with a set of interview probes and questions that have been crafted in the light of a definite theoretical perspective, s/he uses an inter view schedule that is semi-structured at most. Completely closed questions, as found in a questionnaire or fully structured quantified interview schedule, will not be used by even the most doctrinaire neo-positivist. Hence, within the qualitative framework of biographical and family history methods, serendipity in data collection with the opportunity for the respondent to digress along channels relevant to the topic at hand will remain a desired option in even the most formally designed interview schedule. Furthermore, in a hypothesis-testing mode of analysis, expectations can be disconfirmed, implying a subsequent reformulation of ideas. To put it another way, in the neo-positivist approach, after deducing, one must induce.

Realism and neo-positivism also share a common view towards 'objective truth'; that is, that such a creature exists and that the responses of interviewees reflect this truth to some degree, albeit imperfectly. While Realism works in the first instance from interviewees' responses to build a conceptual framework and neo-Positivism uses the responses to evaluate a pre-existing framework, both use real world information in order to develop or refine abstract concepts. In essence these two approaches are complementary. They share a belief in a factual reality that can at least be approached through the collection of empirical information. For both, factual information is the ultimate arbitrator of a common goal – the development and refinement of abstract concepts.

Both approaches share the view that 'the macro' (the structure of the larger society and general social processes) can be apprehended through studying 'the micro' (here, the structure of the family and social processes taking place within individual life and family histories). Individual life or family 'cases' (or, in the case of the narrative approach, the interplay between the interview partners) constitute special instances of a larger whole.

Finally, all three approaches emphasize in one way or another the tension between the subjective viewpoint of an actor and his/her perception of an overarching social structure. This is apparent in the neo-positivist approach where the depiction of structure is central and is evaluated by the respondents' reporting of their subjective perception of their placement in structure and time. There is a similar tension in the realist approach in which reported subjective perception provides the basic units for generalizing to structure. Finally, the narrative approach is built upon a similar tension but at a different level. The postmodern view of 'structure' held by the narrative approach does not see it as a single reality that may be successively approached as it can be in the realist or neo-positivist approaches, but, nevertheless, 'structure' is real in its consequences. The interplay between the two actors in the interview partnership provides insights into a fluctuating reality of shifting positions and the subjective perceptions of this impermanent structure.

Tensions

There are also quite clearly non-trivial differences between the three approaches in their perspectives and procedures. The inductive model of the realist approach, working from particulars to generalizations, contrasts with the deductive, hypothesis-testing bent followed by the neo-positivist approach. These lead to highly contrasting approaches to empirical research. The realist ideal centres around unfocused methods of data collection and a grounded theory mode of analysis that emphasizes serendipity and concept development. In contrast, the neo-positivist approach implies much more controlled methods of data collection that focus on specific topic areas and theory-testing modes of analysis.

Realists and neo-positivists both see 'interview effects' – variations in the courses of interviews caused by the interplay of situational factors in the interview – as idiosyncratic 'static' that must be controlled or minimized in order to prevent the obstruction of the interviewees' ability to give their perceptions in a pure form. For the narrative approach, however, the reverse holds. The interview situation, in particular the interplay between interviewed and interviewer, *is* the core source of information. Realist and neo-positivist life and family *histories* may be contrasted with narrativist life and family *stories*. In the narrative approach it is the manner in which the life or family story develops and is related *during the course of interview*, that which the realist and neo-positivist approaches strive to elim-inate, which provides the essential avenue to understanding. It is the interplay between the interview partners as information is generated that gives clues to social processes and to structures.

This contrast between the realist and neo-positivist ap-proaches and the core of the narrative approach is fundamental. For the narrative approach, there is not a single objective reality that is factual and existing at a level of abstraction beyond the current situation. Reality is (at least potentially) chaotic and in constant flux. What constitutes reality will be dependent upon the temporary joint perceptions generated by the interaction of social actors. Hence, the idea of a single 'meta-reality' which can be apprehended through the use of empirical information is nonsensical to a pure narrativist.

This extreme statement of the narrativist position would be rejected by some who consider themselves to be within the narrative camp. This text, however, will disagree with this self-ascription and argue that a situational view of reality as fluid is an essential part of the narrative approach. Self-labelled narra-tivists who cannot subscribe to a situational view of reality are better seen as either realists or neo-positivists who have been strongly influenced by narrativist insights into the dynamics of the interview.

Prospects

As the above makes clear, there are genuine differences of approach to biographical research. Calls for methodological pluralism within the biographical perspective (for example, Davis 1997) are to be lauded. Pluralism and tolerance, however, does not preclude genuine disagreement. At this point in time, rather than striving for synthesis, perhaps a more reasonable strategy that biographical researchers should follow is to take care to be explicit in the standpoint(s) they adopt in their own work. This introductory chapter has put forward the proposition that there are three basic approaches that can be taken when one is working in the biographical perspective or with family histories – a realist approach that concentrates upon the inductive generation of grounded theory, a neo-positivist approach anchored in the deductive testing of existing theory, and a narrative approach that centres on the situational dynamics of the interview itself. While for the purposes of instruction one can demarcate the 'ideal/typical' differences between these approaches, there is considerable overlap in the world of real research. Researchers tend to be pragmatic, may see the approaches as complementary and will take on board insights from the different approaches. Furthermore, researchers may be unclear about the fundamental approach they have adopted. The result is that in the field practitioners may use procedures that are overlaps of the approaches. Writers following different approaches may employ similar terminology, but with different meanings. This pragmatic, 'cafeteria-style' use of the three approaches does reflect genuine overlaps and complementarity across them. One should however also be cautious and note that the complementarity is not complete. There are real differences of substance between the approaches. Being too blasé in assuming complementarity may be as much a symptom of muddled thinking as eclecticism. In particular, practitioners who adopt a genuine narrative position as their core methodological approach are taking up a position that is incompatible with realists and neo-positivists. It is the practical evaluation of the complementary and contradictory natures of the different approaches to biographical research that will make up the substance of this book.

Appendix – Terminology

The basic terms used within biographical and family history research have undergone an evolution in the 80-odd years since their first inception during the early days of the Chicago School. To prevent confusion, an overview of this terminological evolution will be given here. Originally, life *story* referred to the account given by an individual about his or her life. When this personal account was backed up by additional external sources, such as newspaper reports, official records, photographs, letters or diaries and so on, the validated life story was called a life *history*[8] (Bertaux 1981: 7; Denzin 1995: 117). This concern with triangulation – the validation of narrated life stories through information from additional, preferably quantified, sources has not remained central to most current biographical practice. Nowadays, reflecting the influence of the narrative viewpoint, the meanings of the terms have altered. 'Life history' refers to a series of substantive events arranged in chronological order. Confirmation or validation by external sources is no longer a necessary requirement for a life history. 'Life story' still refers to the account given by an individual, only with emphasis upon the ordering into themes or topics that the individual chooses to adopt or omit as s/he tells the story.

The term 'autobiography' was coined to differentiate between the autobiography – an account given of one's own life – and the biography – an account given of the life of another. The narrative approach, however, contributes the insight that an individual's personal account of their own life, rather than being an unvarying relation of the facts as recollected, is bound to be a tightly edited account for an (possibly hypothetical) intended audience. In composing their life story, the narrator must pick and choose the manner in which they depict their own life in the same manner that a biographer of another person must pick and choose a viewpoint to adopt in relating the life of the other. The distinction between auto/biography becomes blurred, leading to the use of the term 'biography' to describe all accounts of lives – one's own or the lives of others.

Notes

[1] There were some exceptions, such as biographical work in Italy in the 1950s, but this also had come virtually to a stop by the end of the decade (Rammstedt 1995).

[2] My own sociological autobiography fits squarely into this pattern. A secondary student in the southern United States during the height of the civil rights movement and a university student during the late 1960s, I moved from chemistry to sociology seeking wisdom. Instead, I found a discipline that was dry and remote with some rare exceptions. One of the these was *The Sociological Imagination*. The other contemporary examples for me were the early participant

observation studies of work conducted by Donald Roy and studies of community power structures. The only other responsive chords were struck by Myrdal's *An American Dilemma* and some of the classics of the Chicago School. (For an account by Bertaux of his progression along a similar sequence that included *The Sociological Imagination*, see Bertaux, 1981).

[3] Note that in the 1970s, unlike today, the computerized data analysis techniques of large quantitative datasets required expensive mainframe computers whose access was restricted to social scientists located in large educational institutions.

[4] Or *be given*.

[5] Note the double irony of Bogdan's use of the male pronoun here – wrongly applied to represent both (all) genders of the human race and applied to Jane Fry, whose gender identity was mixed.

[6] One should note that biographical and family history techniques, particularly those studying social mobility processes, did not all uniformly distance themselves from the use of quantitative data (Bertaux 1981). Survey data has been collected that spans whole life histories and the analysis of these complex and comparatively rare quantitative life history datasets remains a lively area of social mobility analysis. Furthermore, some proponents of the use of family histories to study social mobility have used data extracted from family histories for quantitative analyses of social mobility (Prandy and Bottero n.d.), sometimes as a justification of the family history approach to social mobility (Jackson and O'Sullivan 1993).

[7] The labels 'realist' and 'narrative' may be less problematic since proponents of these approaches who have forcefully made coherent arguments in their support have used these names consistently. (But note the comments of one self-assigned 'narrativist' who objected to the use of the label 'realist', arguing that it implied that the other approaches were not as 'realistic'.) Given that the current streams of qualitative methods share as a feature of their common origin an aversion to naïve positivism, the label 'neo-positivist' poses the real difficulty. The proponents of this approach have not self-applied any single consistent label, but 'neo-positivist', despite its 'conceptual baggage' and negative connotations for many qualitative researchers, does seem to be an accurate and fair descriptor.

[8] One can note that this original view, in which the facts of the unsubstantiated life story become the life history when confirmed by empirical data, implies a distrust of the subjective and a general positivist orientation in favour of 'objective' factual information.

2

The Historical Context

CONTENTS

*Sociology without history resembles a Hollywood set: great scenes,
sometimes brilliantly painted, with nothing and nobody behind them.*

(Tilly, 1992: 1)

Time and time-related issues are central to the holistic viewpoint that lies at the core of the biographical perspective.
Adopting a biographical perspective leads by definition to an
overview of the whole life course and hence to the historical
events that have shaped a life. A family history spanning only
three generations can easily cover over a century and almost
inevitably will introduce a consideration of the historical events
and social changes that have affected the family over that time
(Bertaux and Thompson 1993). For instance, a 20-year-old student today who collects family history and biographical information from their parents and grandparents will span a period
of living memory that easily stretches back through the Second
World War and the Depression of the 1930s. If the student was
born late in his/her parents lives, say when the mother was
in her early 40s and the father in his 50s and one or both of

the parents in turn had been born late in the lifetime of *their* parents, the period covered can reach to the end of the nineteenth century.

Plummer cogently sums up the centrality of history for the biographical perspective:

> Indeed it is in life history research, as the very name implies, that a proper focus on historical change can be attained in a way that is lacking in many other methods. Such a focus is a dual one, moving between the changing biographical history of the person and the social history of his or her life-span. Invariably the gathering of a life history will entail the subject moving to and fro between the developments of their own life cycle and the ways in which external crises and situations (wars, political and religious changes, employment and unemployment situations, economic change, the media and so forth) have impinged on this. A life history cannot be told without a constant reference to historical change, and this central focus on change must be seen as one of life history's great values. (Plummer 1983: 70)

'History' writ large has impinged upon the life and family histories that people report. The micro/macro interplay between motivations of the individual actor and the social structure that provides opportunities and impediments to ambition and hopes inevitably moves to the fore. 'History' alters the industrial structure and forces people out of previously secure niches as old occupations dwindle or disappear and (hopefully) are replaced by new, different opportunities that require new abilities and skills. A family enterprise created by its founders to provide security for their posterity may turn into a liability as the economic climate alters and the descendants are trapped in a declining economic sector (Jackson and Miller 1983). These broad currents of structural mobility are very real in their consequences. Those who do not appreciate changing parameters of opportunity can find themselves competing in a stagnating job market, perhaps accepting that they are failures when their failure is only partially of their own making. Those who recognize and act on the opening up of new opportunities (or who are just lucky enough to be 'in the right place at the right time') will have better chances for success – a success that they are likely to ascribe to their own efforts and initiative.

'History' can also cause discontinuities – structural changes, and the movements that they force, will create disjunctures beyond a simple game of 'musical chairs' as a person switches from an old position to a new one. People may shift and change repeatedly before a new niche is found (if it ever is). In terms of mobility research the instability created by structural mobility when people are forced by circumstances to leave old positions and seek new ones can cause an additional amount of shifting between jobs whose net effect is a balance – so-called exchange mobility. Wars cause people to break their normal routines and move temporarily into the military or into 'defence' industries. Winning or losing wars, and their consequences, change economies and, hence, also alter opportunity structures and mobility patterns. Recessions cause redundancies and the failures of businesses. Major policy changes or events analogous to major policy changes force people to move jobs or render untenable accepted channels of mobility (Payne 1987). 'Equality' policies, such as the broadening of educational opportunities, open up new channels. Similarly, the reversal of 'equality' policies can be anticipated to have an equivalent, though opposite, effect.

Taking sociological research as an example, a salient and largely unrecognized result of this neglect is the failure to appreciate how often empirical social mobility results obtained in the postwar decades depend upon the era of their collection. Mobility research was not carried out on a large scale until the post-World War II period of economic prosperity and the expansion of white collar strata. Much of what is 'known' about social mobility today may only apply to the immediate postwar period and may not continue to hold if alternative conditions less conducive to upward mobility pertain (Goldthorpe 1985). A base assumption of the 'status attainment' model is implied in its name – that it is normal to attain a higher social position, not to lose one. The predominance of meritocratic achievement (as indexed by educational attainment for example) over ascription, the benefit that comes from advantaged social origins, may only hold when the proportion of higher positions is expanding. While education may be an effective mechanism for allocating new social positions, it may not be as effective as a mechanism for retaining social standing in a context of shrinking opportunities. At the turn of the millennium we may have entered a time of reversal of the postwar trends of upward

mobility, with a consequent re-evaluation of the basic parameters of mobility research (Thompson 1997). The use of the
biographical perspective and the family history approach to the
study of social mobility have been put forward as means of
incorporating a historical perspective (Bertaux and Thompson
1997).

The biographical perspective leads one almost automatically
to consider the effects of time as people tell about the events
that have affected their own lives as they have aged. That the
effects of the passage of time and historical events is central to
the biographical perspective is taken as self-evident. Nevertheless, the interplay of personal ageing, maturation and eventual decline with the broader societal currents of social change
and historical events has remained an undertheorized portion
of biographical research. This lack of coherent development has
held back the evolution of the biographical perspective. The
balance of this chapter will attempt to integrate conceptual
treatments of time that come from a variety of traditions.

Age and the Life Course; Cohorts and Generations; Historical Trends; and Period Effects

The facts of ageing, and eventual death, supply one of the main
engines of social change in any society. As Ryder stated in his
classic article, 'The lives and deaths of individuals are, from the
societal standpoint, a massive process of personnel replacement, which may be called "demographic metabolism" ' (Ryder
1965: 843). The individual members of any ruling elite or
oligarchy, no matter how entrenched it may be, are prey to
mortality. To put it bluntly, the members of even the most
secure of ruling classes all die eventually. As they inevitably are
replaced by other individuals, at least the possibility of change
opens (Mannheim 1952). This fundamental source of potential
change applies to all levels of a society. New cohorts are born
into new times. Their fundamental socialization during childhood and early maturity takes place in an environment that can
be different in many respects from that experienced by earlier
birth cohorts. 'Each new cohort makes fresh contact with
the contemporary social heritage and carries the impress of the
encounter through life. This confrontation has been called the

intersection of the innovative and the conservative forces in history' (Ryder 1965: 846). The historical events experienced by a birth cohort can give it a distinct character and affect both the later life chances of its individual members and how they react to subsequent events (Riley et al. 1988). In these senses, membership in a given birth cohort can affect one's life chances and behaviour dramatically. The significance of this has not been appreciated. Independently of other social structural features, age or, to be more exact, membership in a specific cohort generation can be considered a structural variable of equal significance to other major structural variables, such as class, gender or ethnic group.

When one begins to take the consideration of time seriously, it quickly becomes evident that the interplay between ageing, cohort generation membership and the effects of historical events and trends upon society and social processes has been under-appreciated and deserves closer attention from social scientists (Rindfleisch 1994). The literature on ageing and generational change has not developed systematically and can be characterized more as scattered across a variety of social science disciplines rather than being interdisciplinary (Pilcher 1994). Despite significant and high profile contributions to the area (for example, Mannheim 1952; Eisenstadt 1956; Marias 1970 on Ortega) development has not been cumulative. While ageing is a structural effect at least as significant as class or social development, the core work in the area (for example, Ryder, 1965; Riley, 1973; Riley et al., 1988) has been relegated largely to the sub-area of the sociology of ageing and the elderly. This has led in biographical research to much theoretically misconceived work and analyses fraught with basic conceptual errors (Riley 1973). Studies that purport to use either age or change over time show a tendency to conflate four analytically distinct types of phenomena: *age and life course effects; cohort or generational effects; historical trends; and period effects.*

Riley (1973) has identified two of the basic faults of this type: the *ageing fallacy*[1] and the *generational fallacy.* In the ageing fallacy, differences between individuals of different ages are attributed to the effects of growing older. The potential fallacy is that the age-related difference may be caused completely or in part, not by age, but by the point in time that people were born.[2] For instance, a worsening in health with increasing age might be (correctly) attributed to growing older. It is possible, however, that at least part of the loss of health may be due to other causes. For instance, if older cohorts were born during a time of famine or when standards of sanitation and health care were significantly lower than now, their present-day poorer health may reflect a long-term weakening in their physiology or early illnesses rather than simply ageing.

The generational fallacy is the obverse of the same problem. A researcher could conclude that the worse health of older people is due to their being born during times when health care was of a lower standard when really the poorer health of the elderly is due to their age. As Riley (1973) explains, ageing/life course and cohort/generational effects may work either in tandem (it may be that the poorer health of the elderly is due to both their advanced age and poorer health conditions in their past) or work to cancel each other out. For instance, if the younger members of a society had been born during a time of a famine or other health crisis that older people did not have to live through during their childhood, the two could nullify each other to produce apparently no differences in health by age.

'Cross-sectional data' (information collected at only one point in time) cannot resolve these fallacies. Biographical information, since it usually attempts to cover the totality of an individual's experience across their whole lifetime, does allow one to evaluate the relative significance of ageing versus generational effects.[3]

Age and life course effects

Age effects refer to variance in observed phenomena that can be attributed directly to the ageing of individuals. An individual is born and then moves through various stages of life – for example, from infancy, through childhood and adolescence to adulthood, then middle age, old age and eventual death. While there is flexibility in the rate of biological ageing due to physical effects of the environment – such as an earlier onset of puberty in an environment with a rich diet, or old age arriving earlier in an environment where hard labour, ill health or physiological stress is the norm – the process of biological ageing is inexorable.

While ageing is an individual phenomenon, generations or

birth cohorts can age at varying rates. This variation in the rate of ageing can be considered in part to be a social phenomenon (Pilcher 1995)

> As society changes, each new cohort encounters a unique sequence of social and environmental events. Hence the life-course patterns of people in one cohort will differ in some respects from the life-course patterns of other cohorts. In this sense, different cohorts age in different ways. (Riley et al. 1988: 36)

There is also a process of socially determined chronological ageing that is distinct from biological ageing. Chronological age refers to the sequence of social roles or life stages that an individual goes through during their life – the life course (Giele and Elder 1998). Societal expectations about the behaviour appropriate for a given stage of life *institutionalize* the life course – both ordering and regulating individual action. 'The life course is an "institution" in the sense of a set of regulations of a specific dimension of life, namely, its temporal extension' (Kohli 1986b: 272).

> Life courses . . . follow institutionalized *expectation structures* (see Schütze 1981: 67ff). When we look back on our biography or reflect on our future, we usually adopt a basic framework into which we insert our memories and expectations – childhood, schooling, student days, working life, marriage and so forth. *Every* biography is inevitably structured by such sequential patterns to some extent (Alheit 1994: 309–10, emphasis in original).

The physical ageing of an individual is a biological fact, but the labels attached to given chronological ages in the life course and the activities considered appropriate for them are, within some basic physical parameters, quite malleable. For example, adolescence is a distinct stage in the life course; also, however, its very existence as a recognized category is a fairly recent Western phenomenon. The point that marks the onset of middle age can be set as early as the mid-30s or as late as the mid-50s. As norms change, the definition of behaviour that is appropriate for an age-defined strata in the population can alter. For instance, in contrast to 30 years ago, middle-aged individuals in Western societies today practice a lifestyle that shares many aspects with that of younger age strata. As Chanfrault-Duchet (1995: 212–13) points out:

> As dealt with within the context of biographical research, the life-course issue allows one to view the lifetime on the basis of social norms. Kohli (1985) writes about this basis of 'institutionalizaton' of the life course. From such a definition it is possible to draw the following implications (Fischer and Kohli 1987):
>
> (a) social norms delimit phases in the lifetime – temporalizaton (Brose, 1986) – which are related to periods in one's life – chronologization (Fischer et al. 1985);
> (b) the structuration of the life course is closely dependent on social norms . . .;
> (c) there is a standardization of the life course, i.e. a form of control over individuals (Kohli 1988);
> (d) social norms which overdetermine the life course evolve; researchers are then concerned with long- and short-term evolution, a field which in turn opens up to the life course of cohorts (Renn 1987; Tölke 1987);
> (e) the biographical perspective develops *beyond* the linear succession of the life course.

What constitutes a 'normal' life course for an individual both offers opportunities and imposes constraints. Becoming older can open up new legitimate fields of activity at the same time as it closes down others. (Riley et al. 1972: 10; Riley 1986) These opportunities and constraints can be general mores or prevailing views about what is normal behaviour for someone of a certain age or they can be formalized into age-based statutes, such as setting a legal age for consuming alcoholic beverages or voting or imposing a mandatory retirement age. The age point at which a stage of life typically begins and the subsequent duration of the stage can telescope dramatically due to social changes. In contrast to a century ago when puberty, marriage and a lifetime of child-bearing typically followed each other in quick sequence, late-twentieth century Western societies show a much later average age of marriage, a delay before the birth of the first child and a shortened period of child-bearing. Along with this, there is the introduction of some new 'typical' stages into the life course: instead of going directly from child-rearing to an early death, there is a late adult working life after the children have left home, an active retirement that in turn lengthens into a frail decline into institutionalized or home care (see Riley 1986: 169–70).

After the Famine in Ireland, adulthood and marriage for men was linked to the inheritance of land from the father, thus denying full adulthood to many men until late middle age. The use of the term 'boy' to describe older men in rural Ireland who had not yet inherited the family farm was an accurate depiction of their social status rather than a term of endearment (Arensberg and Kimball 1968: 54–6).

The typical sequence of events in the life course can itself alter. For instance, the 'respectable' ordered pattern of gainful employment preceding marriage which is followed by child-bearing may invert. Furthermore, the norms that even determine the existence of stages of a life course can change. In postindustrial Western societies where manufacturing has declined markedly, the old pattern for working-class males of leaving formal education early for an apprenticeship followed by a lifetime of skilled employment has been replaced by the imposition between full-time education and full-time work of a 'limbo' stage consisting of sporadic menial labour interspersed with episodes of 'youth training' and bouts of unemployment[4] (Miller 1998).

Cohort Generations

Significant confusion in terminology has collected around the usage of the terms *generation* and *cohort* (Rindfleisch 1994: 470). The first use of generation is a 'genealogical' one. Here, generation has a strictly familial meaning – the generation is made up of an individual and his/her siblings (perhaps including cousins). The next generation is made up of children of the individual and his/her siblings. The length of time between generations is the gap between the births of the individual and his/her siblings and the subsequent births of their children – usually approximately 30 years[5] (Strauss and Howe 1991). In this 'family' sense, generation is concerned with socialization, the transmission of values within the family and the inheritance of wealth. Some authors argue that this should be the only use of the term 'generation' (for example, Kertzer 1983; Pilcher 1994 and 1995); but to do so would impose an artificial barrier that excludes the other usages that have been made of the term.

A second meaning of generation refers to a block of people born during a specific span of years who are considered distinct from those who precede or come after them. The 'generation' in this sense refers to an *aggregate* – all people born in a given geographical area or political entity during a set period of time – rather than to a true group of related family members. To discriminate from the former usage, generation in this sense can be called a *cohort generation*. The boundaries around a cohort generation are determined by either: (1) the group born during a time period being demographically distinct in some way from those who came before or after; and/or (2) by historical events or experiences that affect the individuals born during that time period more directly than others alive in the society. 'As a result of differential exposure and exclusion due to location in historical time, there exist different social [cohort] generations, each having distinctive world views. This, in turn, leads people of different ages to experience the *same* social and cultural events differently' (Pilcher 1995: 23; also Riley 1998).

The criteria used to define a cohort generation can vary depending upon the subject of the analysis. The strategy, however, remains constant – to capture the maximum amount of time-based variation across the ages of the sample being analysed so as to be able to make substantive links with historical events and experiences. Rindfleisch, making use of Ryder (1965) summarizes the characteristics and significance of a cohort generation:

> A *cohort generation* is a group of persons born during a limited span of years who share a common and distinct social character shaped by their shared experiences through time (Mannheim, 1952; Marias, 1970). Unlike *family generations*, which are based on biological lineages, *cohort generations* are based on shared historical experiences. . . . a cohort generation is a social structural variable akin to social class, race or gender. . . . According to Ryder (1965): 'At a minimum, the cohort is a structural category with the same kind of analytic utility as a variable like social class. Conceptually the cohort resembles most closely the ethnic group: membership is determined at birth, and often has considerable capacity to explain

variance, but need not imply that the category is an organized group (p.847)'. (Rindfleisch, 1994: 470, emphasis in original)

Hence, cohort generations should be considered as significant as other major structural variables such as class, gender, religion or ethnic group (also see Riley et al. 1988).

Perhaps the best-known example of a cohort generation is the so-called 'Baby Boomers' – those born in the United States and western Europe after the Second World War between about 1946 and 1955. The 'Baby Boomer'/'Vietnam' generation was defined by the demographic effects[6] of history. American fertility was suppressed by the economic Depression of the 1930s and the disruption of mobilization during the Second World War; it then rose when the return of the soldiers coincided with a prolonged period of postwar prosperity. The unusually high birthrates of the immediate postwar period produced a demographic 'lump' in the population – the 'Baby Boom' – that has profound effects for society as the 'lump' ages and works its way up the age pyramid. The 'Baby Boomers' were the archetype for Easterlin's (1978) hypotheses that birth cohorts of significantly different sizes will cause imbalances within the social structure as they move through their life courses. The 1950s were characterized by overcrowded primary schools, as the 1960s saw an unprecedented expansion in higher education that was driven in part by the sheer numbers qualified to enter universities and colleges. The proportionate imbalances between age strata will induce the social structure to change in either minor or major ways so as to accommodate the new proportions. Western governments currently are desperately seeking ways of curtailing or privatizing health care and social security systems as they anticipate dramatic rises in the proportions of dependent elderly in the coming decades.

As well as causing changes in social structure, demography can contribute to cultural changes. American culture in the 1950s can be termed a child-centred culture centred around the 'Baby Boomer' cohort generation. This is turn gave way to the youth-obsessed 'counter-culture' of the 1960s when the same generation began to enter adulthood and to the gross materialism of the Reagan/Thatcher period when they reached their peak earning years.

As well as being demographically unique, the 'Baby Boomers' also are defined by history as the so-called 'Vietnam generation' in the United States, since their identity was confirmed by unique historical experiences, most notably that they reached young adulthood during the Vietnam War and made up both the majority of the troops who fought and the dissidents who opposed the war. This cohort's experience of the Vietnam War, an event common to the whole society, differed radically from the rest of the population because it was the generation subject to military conscription.

While there are not hard and fast criteria for determining cohort generations or setting the dates that will be the dividing lines between them, some general principles do apply to identifying cohort generations. Firstly, there is the principle of *coincidence*. If a number of phenomena coincide, the creation of a cohort generation is made more likely. The above is a prime example where an initial demographic identity coincides some 20 years later with the historical experience of the Vietnam War, the cultural and political ramifications of that war and the rise of the 'counter-culture' of the 1960s.

Secondly, societies can experience a profound political or social transformation that sets up a 'watershed' that determines three cohort generations:

- a *before* cohort generation – those born far enough before the break point to have reached full adulthood prior to the change;
- a *transition* cohort generation – those who are adolescents or young adults at the point of transition whose lives begin under the old system but whose main secondary socialization, education and early labour market experiences take place during the time of transition. The events that take place during adolescence and early adulthood tend to be the definitive experiences for determining political and cultural identity, so this cohort generation often is set apart from the others by a 'revolutionary' consciousness that may persist throughout the lifetimes of its members;
- an *after* cohort generation – those who are born after the transition and whose complete life experience takes place under the new regime. For this cohort, the vivid, life-defining

experiences of the previous cohort generations appear as dead history that took place in a time of antiquity.

Post-colonial societies supply good examples of cohort generations defined by these watershed transformations: a before cohort generation that grew up and was established in the old colonial system that existed prior to independence; an independence cohort generation that carried out the struggle for freedom; and a postindependence generation that was born and grew up after the struggle was over. It is probable that 1989 will come to constitute a similar cohort generation-defining watershed for eastern and central Europe.

While all the members of a cohort generation may have lived through the same events at approximately the same ages, it does not necessarily follow that all of the members of the cohort generation will have developed the same consciousness about the defining events of their generation. Each person alive at the time will have their own recollections of how the defining events of their generation affected them. These personal remembrances will be just that – individuated recollections of how 'history' impinged upon one's own trajectory or life course. These may resemble the experiences of others, but will be unique to the person. In contrast, that which can be common to a cohort generation is 'collective memories' – common perspectives or interpretations of the generation's joint experience that were constructed as part of a *social* interaction with other co-members of the generation who were going through the same experiences (Schumann and Scott 1989). For instance, the 'counter-culture' experienced by many of the 'Baby Boomer' generation was a common set of perspectives, feelings and behaviours that were built up through a process of interaction with other members of the generation. Similarly, others of the same generation who experienced combat in Vietnam first-hand developed a common perspective on the experience that persists until today.

As the above implies, different strata within a cohort generation may have utterly different collective memories. These different strata within a cohort generation, experiencing different aspects of the same defining events and developing varying sets of collective memories have been termed *generational units* (Riley et al. 1988). The characteristics that cause generational units to experience the key events of their generation in different ways are likely to be divisions with the cohort generation induced by structural variables such as class, sex, race or ethnic group. In that way, the structural effects of age/cohort generation interact with other major structural variables (Laufer and Bengtson 1974). For example, combat soldiers in Vietnam were predominantly working class and disproportionately black, the so-called 'hippies' haled from privileged upper-middle-class backgrounds.

The length of a generation has been a topic of considerable debate (Rindfleisch 1994). In fact, this is a false debate reflecting the confusion between the familial view of generations and cohort generations. The time span of a familial generation is the gap in time between the birth of children into a family and the children themselves having offspring. The time span that defines a cohort generation is more plastic and can vary widely depending upon circumstances – the demographic characteristics or historical experiences that render a particular cohort unique. Hence, different cohort generations may cover time spans of varying lengths. Individuals born during years that are the most demographically or historically unique can be said to make up the 'core' of a cohort generation (Pilcher 1995). People born during years when the birth cohort does not have any atypical demographic characteristics or uniquely identifying historical experiences might fall into a 'limbo' between generations.[7] In effect, the generation here is a birth cohort whose boundaries are defined by demographic characteristics and/or historical events.

Cohorts

Many analyses based upon cross-sectional survey data claim to incorporate age as a 'structural' variable by basing their analytic strategy upon the use of cohorts. The surveyed individuals are divided into groups based upon age. Where age cohort analyses differ from analyses based upon cohort generations is that the age division is an arbitrary one. The criterion for division is merely the allocation of a sufficient number of individuals to each cohort that is deemed necessary for a statistically reliable analysis (Rindfleisch 1994). The groupings are either by decades, ten-year age blocks, or by an arbitrary division into a number of age-based categories; in each instance the number of categories is determined mainly by a need to have sufficient cases in each category.

Arbitrary division into age-based categories in which the categories are determined solely by the needs of a probabilistically based analysis is poor sociological practice. Unless the time-dependent variables of interest increase or decrease regularly across the whole age span of the sample without any significant breaks, an arbitrary division is likely to miss or obscure significant variation. The arbitrary age categories will only capture significant variation if their cut-off points happen by chance to match significant points in the data. Returning to the 'Baby Boomer' example used above, one can note that an arbitrary division into birth decades would split the cohort generation – almost half would go into the 1940–49 age cohort and be conflated with the very different group of those born during the height of the Second World War. In order to allow for a genuine testing of hypotheses based upon historical events or trends, a much better analytic practice is to use sociologically informed cohort generations as the age-based categories for analysis.

Historical trends

As noted above, unique historical or demographic events will define cohort generations. The 'Baby Boomer'/'Vietnam' cohort generation was defined by the demographic effects of history with the distinct demographic identity of the cohort generation, then confirmed by unique historical experiences, most notably a southeast Asian war. The unique demographic and historical effects that define a cohort generation will appear in time-based analyses as 'peaks' or 'troughs' in data. For instance, entering the labour market for the first time during a time of labour shortage or labour surplus can have negative or positive effects upon careers that will persist across whole lifetimes (Easterlin 1978).

Not all historical effects are so idiosyncratic however. Much social change will be in the form of a regular increase or decrease in a phenomenon; for example, the gradual decline of the agricultural sector that has been experienced or is being experienced by almost all societies. Attitudes or mores can change as well as structure. For instance, the economic and political position of women has altered radically over the last century steadily towards more inclusiveness so that now women finally may be approaching complete equity in the economic and political structures. Changes in attitudes towards women's inclusion have gone in tandem with structural changes. The rate of change may wax or wane over comparatively short spans, but the direction will remain constant. As Sorokin pointed out in his classic work on social mobility some 70 years ago, trends cannot continue indefinitely (Sorokin 1959 [1927]). Social trends, however, can continue across decades or centuries before they play themselves out. A true historical trend should appear in an analysis as a regular increase or decrease in an observed phenomenon that is independent of age or cohort generational effects. Being more lasting, a true historical trend by its nature will have more sociological significance than temporary, though significant, historical events.

Period effects

While qualitatively different from the above, period effects are of significance for the analysis of time- or history-based phenomena. Period effects are caused by conditions pertaining at the time of data collection (Schumann and Scott 1989), and do not indicate true historical trends or genuine 'peaks' or 'troughs' in a phenomenon. They can be considered analogous to temporary 'static' that might obscure a true signal. Period effects can particularly become a factor affecting results when information is collated together from a series of studies which took place at intervals over a span of time. If special conditions affected the responses given at one or more times, this could be wrongly interpreted as a fact of substantive significance. The social context in which the data are being collected may be temporarily altered at one particular time point, producing a false 'glitch'. For example, if one of a series of studies collecting information on the public's opinion of the honesty of politicians happens to take place at the same time as a major political scandal, a temporary drop in the public's estimation of politicians may result. Unless the analyst is aware that the drop is a temporary fluctuation in public opinion, it may be wrongly considered a more permanent phenomenon.

Any special conditions that happen to pertain at the time of the collection of information can fall within the ambient of a period effect. This could be something as mundane as an alteration or lapse in data collection procedure. For instance, apparently minor changes in survey-question wording some-times can have major effects upon responses. A core premise of the narrative approach within the biographical perspective, that the interplay between the interviewer and interviewee means that the information collected during the taking of a life story is malleable, can be seen within this typology as a kind of 'period effect'.

The *fallacy of proportional representation* (Riley 1973: 43–44) is a period effect based upon the observation that differently sized cohorts can shift *overall* empirical findings. For example, con-temporary crime figures from the United States have recorded a number of drops in violent crime, for which incumbent politicians are quick to claim credit. Instead of resulting from direct causes such as more effective policing, however, the drops may be no more than an artefact of cohort size. Recently, the size of the cohort of young males in the United States has fallen. Since members of this group are the prime perpetrators of certain types of violent crime, the drop in crime rates may only reflect a drop in the number of perpetrators. When the size of the cohort rises again, so may the crime figures.

Summary

This chapter began by noting the lack of a cumulative and con-gruent treatment of time-related concepts within the biograph-ical perspective and moved on to discuss the need to establish a historical context in which to place the empirical results of bio-graphical studies. It was noted that apparent 'historical effects' can be the conflation of three separate time-related phenomena. Figure 2.1 displays the relationships between the three different types of phenomena graphically.[8]

First, *'age'* or *'maturation' effects*, in fact, are not true 'historical effects' at all, but rather the moving of a given cohort through

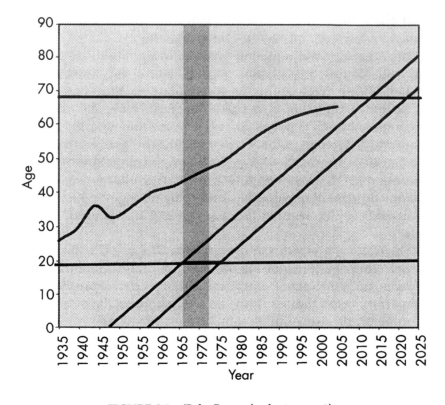

FIGURE 2.1 *'Baby Boomer' cohort generation*

the life course – a sequence of events common to all cohorts over a lifetime. Ageing appears in the figure as the straight lines running diagonally from the bottom left to the upper right. Riley describes this diagonal metaphorically as an 'escalator'. 'An escalator suggests how, as people age, they move *diagonally* upward with age and *across* time (in this figure of speech, they move through different social scenery[9]).' (Riley, 1998: 39) [Italics in original] For instance, those born in the year 1946 (aged '0' in 1946) are 18 in 1964 and will be aged 79 in the year 2025. The two horizontal lines running across illustrate life course points that are important for all, reaching the age of 18 and reaching mandatory retirement age at age 65.[10] Age 18 is a particularly important point in the life course for the male half of the 1946 birth year, since they then became eligible for military conscription just at the start of the United States's involvement in Vietnam. Apparent differences between younger and older groups due solely to age will evaporate as the younger cohort grows older.

Second, *true historical trends* are conceived of as gradual shifts in the level or distribution of a structural feature of a society; such as the amounts and types of educational attainment, or the breakdown into industrial sectors or occupational categories. Here, the curved line illustrates a historical trend – the female labour participation rate in the United States over the period 1935 to 2005.[11] Throughout the period, the participation rate for women has risen steadily, from approximately 26 percent in 1935 to a projected 62 percent in the year 2005. (The 'bump' in the line for the years of the Second World War reflects the temporary mobilization of women into the labour force during the War. This 'bump' is a good example of a temporary 'period effect'.)

Third, there are *true cohort generation effects*, demographic, sociological and political experiences unique to a given cohort, which cause it to differ in terms of both substantive position and consciousness from preceding and following cohorts. The 'Baby Boomer' cohort generation appears as the diagonal band of those born between 1946 and 1955. One can note how the diagonal band depicting this cohort generation intersects with the shaded vertical bar for the years 1965–1972, the period of the Vietnam War, at the point at which the 'Baby Boomers' were in their late teens and early 20s.

Since different units within a cohort generation may perceive or be affected differently by historical events, and the differences in these perceptions may vary by structural characteristics such as gender, social class or ethnic group, cohort generations link crucially to social structure. Each society can have cohort generations unique to itself, the exact criteria and timing of which may not match those for other societies. Nevertheless, the rate of contemporary social change is such that each present-day society, whether 'modern' or 'postmodern', will have distinct cohort generations. Those adopting a biographical perspective in their research need to discriminate between the different types of time-related effects. In particular, the need to establish cohort generations based upon socially relevant criteria is a universal for those wishing to place their biographical work into a genuine historical context.

Notes

[1] In fact, Riley labels this as the *life course fallacy*, but *ageing fallacy* is a more correct term to use. As discussed below, life course refers to the progression through a number of stages during a lifetime, rather than simply growing older.

[2] To phrase it more exactly, the *cohort generation* into which they were born. The meaning of cohort generation is discussed below.

[3] One must inject a note of caution here. Most biographical information is collected at only one time (the present) with the individual being asked to tell about their life history up to that point in time. Hence, strictly speaking it is a form of cross-sectional information and cannot provide iron-clad protection against the ageing and generational fallacies. What would be required for a definitive resolution to the possibility of these fallacies is true longitudinal information gathered over a lengthy span of time so that, if trends over age do exist, they may be observed. Furthermore, in case a real difference does exist between cohorts or generations defined by different times of birth, the information must be collected for at least two distinct age cohorts so that the difference can be observed or at least ruled out.

[4] Full-time work when it is eventually attained is likely to be semi-skilled and 'flexible' without the security of tenure.

[5] The gap of 30 years between familial generations does seem to be confirmed empirically. Family trees stretching back over many generations often do exhibit a regular 30-year cycle of birth to reproduction of the next generation in the family.

[6] Especially pronounced in the United States.

[7] The pace of events and social change in modern times makes the possibility of a 'limbo' generation to whom nothing of note occurred extremely unlikely. In the past, however, for example during the Middle Ages in Europe, this might have been the case (or one could admit the possibility of 'cohort generations' that covered a very long span of time).

[8] Figure 2.1 is an adaptation of Riley's figures that depict the interplay between ageing, cohort progression and historical time. For examples, see Riley et al. (1972), Riley (1986) and Riley (1998).

[9] The second metaphor being used by Riley here, 'moving through different social scenery' refers to the observation that – since social structure does not remain static over time, but instead changes – as people age the social structures in which they live are altering.

[10] Other important points in the life course, such as completing education or beginning a family, cluster around a definite and fairly narrow age band for most but are not associated with a single year. It would be difficult to illustrate these with a single line in the figure, so they have not been included.

[11] Source: United States Bureau of the Census (1957; 1983; and 1996). The female participation rate for 2000–2005 is a Census projection.

3

Collecting and Organizing Family Histories

CONTENTS

'You may choose your friends, but you can't choose your family.'

This chapter will be a departure from the previous two. Rather than discussing conceptual issues, it will centre upon the collection and application of family histories, making use of the 'Social Genealogies Commented on and Compared' techniques pioneered by Daniel Bertaux (1995). These practical family history exercises are designed to sensitize the student to the interplay between the individual and the wider social structure in which they are embedded and to provide a lead-in to interviewing and the approaches to analysis followed by those who adopt the biographical perspective and collect life stories.

Announcements of 'the death of the family' are premature and alarmist. With the exception of abandoned babies, everyone begins their lives within a family of some sort. Even if these early connections are severed early in an individual's personal life history, as with the case of orphans, most people create new families of their own. Single parenthood, voluntarily childless couples, couples (heterosexual or homosexual) living together without formally sanctioned ties, divorce, 'serial monogamy' and so on can be considered different forms of family life rather than qualitatively different phenomena. The greater variety of family types in present (post)modern times can be considered no more a sign of the demise of the family than the century-old eclipse of the traditional agricultural extended family by the rise of the atomized nuclear family.[1] Families remain an important feature of (post)modern life and are of great importance and influence for most, if not all, people (Bertaux-Wiame 1993). 'Family is still the principal channel for the transmission of languages, names, land and housing, local social standing, and religion; and beyond that . . . also of social values and aspirations, domestic skills, and . . . taken-for-granted ways of behaving' (Thompson 1997: 43).

Families continue to provide emotional support and are the main source of primary relationships. It may be fashionable to deride the functionalist assertion that families play an essential 'emotional/affective' role in providing close primary contacts, but that role remains no less essential.

> Within . . . contexts of [urban] protracted generalized competition, kinship ties take on new meanings. Families become essential as places where physical, intellectual and moral energies get differentially produced and renewed, as units for strategic thinking and resource mobilization, and as protective nets against harsh competition. To caricature: without a good home, children will fail in the competition for good school grades; youths will fail in the quest for a good job, or for a valuable partner; adults, men and women, will not be able to stand the pressure of work relationships and to play the game of the struggle for life. (Bertaux 1995: 74)

Families act as an important link between individuals and the larger social structure in which they are embedded. Riley calls this:

> [T]he 'two-step flow' of influence . . . that macro-level forces exert full influence on individuals as they are screened and reinforced through primary groups. . . . Thus, Elder (1974) found that the effects of the Depression on the lives of children varied with the degree of economic deprivation of their *families*; or that the reper-

cussions of *family* patterns and resources were more traumatic for children who were younger, rather than older, at the time of the Depression (Elder and Rockwell 1979). . . . *meso-level structures often mediate* the 'intersection of personal and social history'. (Riley 1998: 44 45, emphasis in original)

Families also constitute the primary mechanism for the transmission of resources between generations. This transmission of resources can be substantial. Parents, of course, provide material support for their offspring while they are children. Inheritance of property or wealth is a prime mechanism for the transmission of wealth between generations. Traditionally, young adults have been an 'insurance policy' for aged adults, providing support during their old age. While the direction of support between generations can be seen as reversing itself in more recent times with the older generation transferring resources to young adults in the forms of college tuition and help in setting up house, the care given by family members to their elderly members remains significant (and has a definite material value), particularly as the welfare state provisions of the mid-twentieth century undergo retrenchment.

The point is that the harder the generalized competition, the more important will be the resources that individuals (and nuclear families) can receive from their parents and kin, be they economic resources, cultural resources, physical resources, connections or other kinds of trump cards in the tough game of urban life. . . . Hence, the importance of the transmissions, between generations, of various kinds of resources . . .; and the value of an instrument that would allow one to focus on such transmissions. (Bertaux 1995: 74–75)

The transfer of resources between generations can take forms other than that of the transfer of material capital. Families can act as reservoirs of knowledge and skills – so-called *cultural capital* – which they may transmit to their younger generation. The existence of cultural resources within the family makes for more efficient exploitation of cultural opportunities available in the wider society. A clear-cut example of this would be the ability of educated parents to assist their children's own progress through the formal system of education. This ability can take many forms, from the provision of books and magazines in the home, through practical help with school assignments and homework, to inculcating a middle class accent and 'proper' manners.

A family's status and position also can constitute resources that can be passed between generations – so-called *social capital* (Bertaux and Bertaux-Wiame 1997). 'Social capital' is 'resources that are embedded in sets of social relations' (Elliott 1997: 211). A parent's business connections can be exploited in order to provide an employment opportunity for a child – for example, guaranteeing favourable treatment during a job interview. Aristocratic or upper-class families may have a collective family memory of 'service' or ruling that spurs its younger members into positions of power which they see as their 'natural right' or 'duty' (Muxel 1993: 192–6).

'Social capital' may be most significant in its effects as *negative* social capital. For instance, being a member of an ethnic or racial group that is subject to prejudice or discrimination can leave one open to social and economic handicaps.

Finally, the benefits conferred by the various types of 'capital' will overlap. For instance, staying with the example of education, material wealth can confer educational advantages – a subscription to *National Geographic* or the possession of a family computer with *Encyclopedia Britannica* on CD-rom costs money (as does living in a home large enough for there to be a quiet room for study), to say nothing of the ability to pay tuition fees. There can be similar overlaps with 'social capital' – middle-class parents will see themselves (correctly) as having a social status equivalent to that of their children's teachers, and hence will be able to negotiate more effectively with teachers on their children's behalf.

Exercise 1: Constructing a family history chart

The construction of a family history chart using the techniques of Bertaux's 'Social Genealogies Commented on and Compared' provides a means of collecting information about a family in order to gain insight into the processes of transmission between generations and also a framework for linking family history with an individual's life story.

> In the method of Social Genealogies Commented On and Compared, the unit of observation is not an individual, but a set of life trajectories of individuals (and nuclear families) connected by kinship relations. The basic idea is to define the unit of observation so as to include several generations (at least three), and to have roughly as many persons/couples on [sic] each generation; in short, to define 'rectangular' genealogies. (Bertaux 1995: 75).

Procedure:

Choose a family (it can be your own). Construct a family history chart/diagram which includes:

a) the 'target individual';
b) the siblings (brothers and sisters);
c) the parents;
d) *the parents'* siblings and their spouses (husbands and wives);
e) *all* of their children;
f) the maternal and paternal grandparents;
g) the siblings of the maternal and paternal grandparents.

For example, if you chose your own family with yourself as target, the chart would include:

a) you;
b) your brothers and sisters;
c) your mother and father;
d) your aunts and uncles *and* their husbands and wives;
e) your cousins;
f) all four of your grandparents;
g) all of your great aunts and uncles who were 'blood' relations.

Put the current (target individual's) generation across the bottom, put the parents'/aunts and uncles' generation a level above, and the grandparents' generation at the top. Order each set of siblings

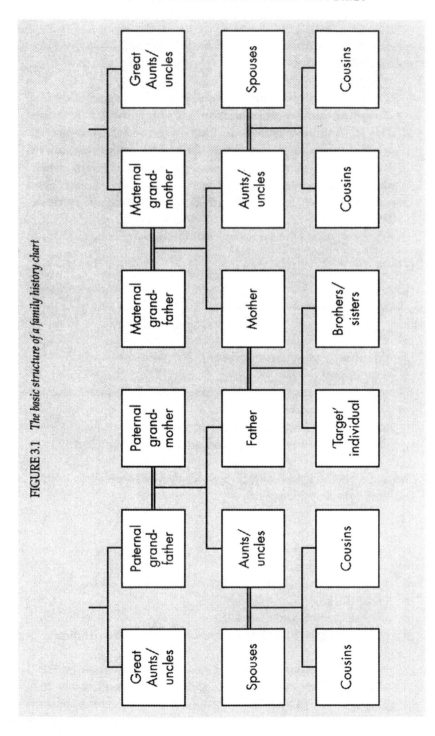

FIGURE 3.1   *The basic structure of a family history chart*

with the oldest on the left and the youngest on the right. For each person on the chart, put the following information into a box as below:

> First name,
> Year of birth, Place of birth
> Highest educational attainment
> First 'real' job
> Most typical job during lifetime
> Present/last location
> *Any other points of note*

Figure 3.1 shows a simplified version of the layout of a family history chart.

Notes/Hints:

1   Many people will choose their own family for this exercise. This is fine. If you are an average age for a university student (that is, in your late teens or early 20s), however, your relatively young age can lead to some problems. Unless all of your brothers, sisters and cousins are older than you, it will be better to select someone from an older generation as the 'target individual'. A lot of the 'action' (for example, World War II) could have taken place in the older generations. Secondly, if you are older than most of your siblings and cousins and select yourself as 'target', the lifetime of many in the youngest generation still will be a matter of anticipation or speculation. Many or most of the younger generation will be too young to have completed education, had any real jobs, or to have been geographically mobile. So, instead of having three complete generations to analyse, you end up with only two-and-a-half generations.

2   Bertaux (1995) recommends a variation in the people about whom information is collected. For (g), instead of the 'siblings of the grandparents', he suggests that information should be collected for the 'parents of the spouses' of aunts and uncles (Bertaux, 1995: 76–7). If his suggestion is followed, the advantage is that information can be obtained for a greater

variety of people. The disadvantage is that it may be difficult to obtain reliable information about these distant relations (great aunts and great uncles by marriage).

3a   Whichever technique is used, try hard to collect all the information for each person and make the charts complete. Any means is acceptable – questioning a variety of relatives, which may require writing or telephoning those who live elsewhere, consulting family or public records and so on. Nevertheless, despite your best efforts it may prove impossible to find out complete information for all your relatives. If after exhausting all avenues and sources, there still is 'missing data', what is not known and for whom it cannot be found out becomes 'data' in itself. That is, there must be a good reason why these facts cannot be collected for some of the relatives – find out the reason;

3b   Conversely, some students will be able to collect high-quality information that goes back *further* than three generations. If you can, there is nothing to prevent you going back to this more distant family history.

4   You may find that setting up the chart so as to allow sufficient spacing for the inclusion of all the family members is difficult. It is a good idea to do a rough layout with just everyone's names before doing the final chart. Have some correction fluid or an eraser handy.

5a   'First "real" job' will be the first genuine employment the person was in. *Not* 'housewife' for women unless they never worked outside the home prior to marriage. The purpose of this item is to have an indication of the person's job status at the beginning of their adult working life.

5b   'Most typical job' will be the job that was most significant for them and/or the job held for most of their life. For a woman, this may be 'housewife'. The purpose of this item is to have an indication of the person's job status throughout the majority of their working life. You may notice interesting patterns of occupational mobility within lives, between generations, or between different branches of the family.

6   'Location' means where they are now (or where they last lived before they died). When compared with 'Place of birth', you may be able to see patterns of migration such as movement from rural to urban areas.

7   'Any other points of note' could include facts such as '*didn't*

complete education due to the Second World War'; 'had to return home when inherited family business'; 'married twice'; 'seriously ill during most of adult life' and so on – whatever seems important that does not fit in elsewhere. If a person made a significant migration during their lifetime (for example, immigrating to the United States or making a major shift from living in a rural area to living in a large city) record this here, giving the age when they migrated.

As an example of what your finished chart may look like, Figure 3.2 is an excerpt from the author's own family chart. Note that only a portion of this family will fit on to a single page.

Exercise 2: 'The Macro in the Micro': Constructing tables from the family history charts

As Riley (1998: 44–5) noted, the family can be an important point of contact between the individual and the larger social structure. The purpose of this second exercise is to demonstrate how the social processes and historical events that affect a whole society can be mirrored in the lives of small units within the greater society, such as a single extended family. Use the information contained in your family chart to provide the 'data' necessary for the tables below. Explanations on how to construct the tables are given here, but these explanations should be considered as guidelines only. Places differ from each other, and you may want to modify the suggestions below to suit 'your' location better. Hence, the exact procedures for constructing the tables and collecting information from the family charts which your class will follow should be agreed by the group prior to building the tables.

As you develop the tables, think about whether the patterns that appear in them are typical. Obviously, a single family (even the 'extended' collection of nuclear families displayed on your chart) cannot display all of the significant social processes in operation in your society, but some aspects of the family's experience should reflect larger social processes that have affected the society as a whole – even if they are only 'the exception that proves the rule'. In

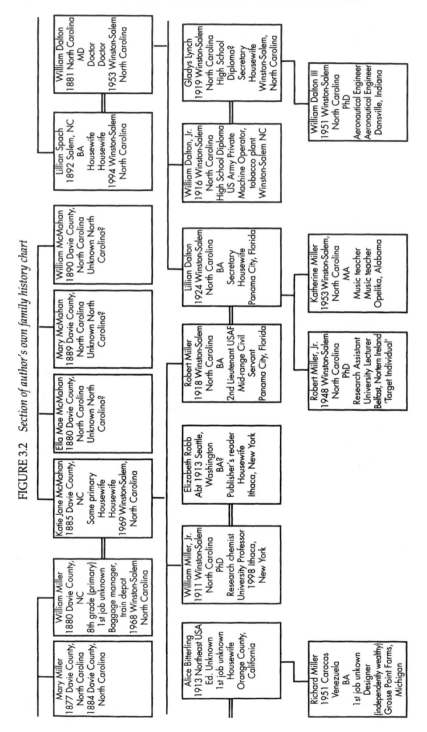

FIGURE 3.2 Section of author's own family history chart

order to get a broader view of the representativeness of your family, after each person has developed their own tables, these will be brought together and collated into a single 'master set' of tables for the whole class.

First example – 'Change in fertility'

Taking each of the three generations in your chart in turn, calculate the average number of children born to the adult women in each generation by dividing the total number of children born alive by the total number of adult (aged 15 or older) women and enter the results in a table like that of Table 3.1 below:

Table 3.1   *Fertility of generation*[1]

	Grandparents	Parents	Target ind.
Number of children/ woman	5.8	4.1	3.3

[1] Numbers are the averaged reports from the family history charts of 20 students at the Queen's University of Belfast, 1998.

The pattern likely to appear for most families will be a drop in the average number of children for each generation.[2] Since the intention is to obtain an indication of the fertility of the whole generation, note that *all* adult women should be included in the calculation, even if they were not in a position where they would be expected to have children; for example, all single women (even nuns) should be included.[3] Since the measure is based upon women rather than couples, single mothers can be included and problems in calculation that would be caused by people divorcing or being widowed and then remarrying are avoided.[4]

Second example – 'Change in education'

Taking each of the three generations in your chart in turn, code the educational attainment of each person into the CASMIN schema and enter the enter the number of family members at each level of educational attainment in a table like that of Table 3.2:[5]

Table 3.2   *Education of generation*[1]

Educational level[2]	Generation		
	Grandparents	Parents	Target ind.
LT minimum	81%	17%	1%
Minumum	16%	43%	9%
Minimum + vocational	–	3%	2%
Some secondary beyond minimum	1%	19%	23%
Secondary + vocational	–	6%	10%
Secondary + academic	2%	8%	26%
'Maturity'	–	2%	8%
Lower tertiary	–	1%	10%
Higher tertiary	–	1%	7%
Postgraduate	–	–	4%
Total	100%	100%	100%

[1] Percentages are based upon the educational distributions reported from the family history charts of 36 students at the Universiti Kebangsaan Malaysia, 1997.
[2] CASMIN Educational Codes (König et al. 1987).
  1   Less than legal minimum schooling
  2   Minimum schooling
  3   Minimum + vocational qualification/training
  4   Some (secondary) education beyond minimum
  5   Secondary + vocational qualification/training
  6   Secondary + some academic qualification
  7   'Maturity' – education sufficient for university entry
  8   Lower tertiary – some third-level education
  9   Higher tertiary – university-level education
  10 Postgraduate qualification

Since a trend over the last century throughout the globe has been increasing levels of education, a pattern similar to that shown in the table is likely to appear – generally low levels of educational attainment in the 'grandparents' generation that rise for each subsequent generation. A pattern that often appears across the generations within the family history charts is a 'knock on' effect of a small amount of educational attainment in the 'grandparent' generation: a pattern of increasing educational attainment across generations centred in some branches of the family tree only, which seems to be presaged by grandparents who had somewhat more than the minimum education typical for their generation. Does such a pattern appear in your family history chart?

Third example – 'Geographic mobility'

Taking each of the three generations in your chart in turn, use each person's information on 'place of birth' and 'present/last location' to produce tables of geographic mobility like those of Tables 3.3a and 3.3b below. For each person, categorize their 'place of birth' by whether it was 'Urban' or 'Rural' or, alternatively, somewhere in the 'Rest of the world'. Then categorize their 'present/last' location similarly, but with one exception – if their 'present/last' location is the same as their place of birth, record them as 'same place'. For people with a 'Rural' place of birth, 'same place' would be living/last lived in the same area (within several kilometres of their birthplace). For 'Urban' origin, 'same place' would be either living in the same town as at birth or, if they were born in a large city, living in the same area of that large city. For example, an American born in New York City in Brooklyn who was currently living in Brooklyn, would be recorded as 'Urban' origin and 'Same place' for present/last location. Someone born in Brooklyn but now living in the Queens borough of New York City would *not* be recorded as 'Same place' for present/last location but rather as 'Urban' origin and 'Urban' present/last location.

Table 3.3a   *Geographic mobility, basic format*

	Present/last location			
Origin	Same place	Urban	Rural	Rest of World
Urban				
Rural				
Rest of world				

The basic format of the geographic mobility table should be seen as a template which can be modified to fit the circumstances of the geographic mobility patterns that will have affected your families. For instance, does your area have a large centrally located city that will have exerted a significant influence on patterns of geographic movement? Do you live in a country that supplies many immigrants to other parts of the world or itself experiences high levels of in-migration from elsewhere? Considerations such as these may lead your class to decide to add in extra geographic location categories. The province of Northern Ireland, for instance, is dominated by the city of Belfast and has lost much of its population to immigration to other parts of the world, especially Britain. This led students constructing a geographic mobility table for Northern Ireland to modify the basic format by breaking 'Urban' into two categories, 'Belfast' and other 'N.I. urban' and to separate 'Britain' out of the 'Rest of the world' category. Table 3.3b shows the result:

Table 3.3b *Geographic mobility, target individual's generation, Northern Ireland*[1,2]

| Origin | Present/last location | | | | | | |
	Same place	Belfast	N.I. Urban	N.I. Rural	Britain	Rest of World	Total
Belfast	12%	21%	29%	25%	13%	12%	28%
N.I. urban	68%	2%	17%	4%	4%	6%	12%
N.I. rural	33%	2%	16%	28%	11%	11%	42%
Britain	43%	0%	0%	7%	44%	6%	12%
Rest of world	52%	0%	7%	11%	4%	26%	6%
Total	–	9%	25%	35%	19%	14%	100%

[1] Percentages are derived from the family history charts of 20 students at the Queen's University of Belfast, 1998.
[2] Except for the right-hand 'Total' column, all percentages are row percentages, summing to 100% along rows.

The modal age of the 'target individual's' generation in Table 3.3b will be people who were aged in their 40s in 1998.[6] During the lifetimes of the people in the table, Northern Ireland was urbanizing, but the city of Belfast itself experienced a population decline as people moved out to suburban areas. At the same time, the province as a whole continued to display its historical pattern of emigration to Britain and other parts of the world. These features appear in the table. Taking the top row – those born in Belfast – as an example: large proportions of those born in Belfast now live outside the city – 29 per cent and 25 per cent in other urban and rural areas in Northern Ireland respectively and this reflects the relative shrinkage of the population in Belfast. As one would expect, the contrary pattern is absent – few born outside Belfast presently live within the city. Also, reflecting the steady drain of out-migration from the province that persists up to the present day, significant proportions of those born in Northern Ireland are shown as now living either in Britain or elsewhere outside of the province.[7]

The patterns of migration or geographic movement identified in your tables will depend upon the parameters affecting your families and of course may vary from those found above. One feature you might wish especially to watch out for in your chart will be the presence of 'mobile families'. Often one member of a family, perhaps an older sibling, can act as a 'pioneer', moving to a new location. Once they are established, by virtue of their knowledge of the new location and practical help such as assistance with fares or finding jobs for their relations, they provide a bridge for the migration of other family members to the same place. Can you find evidence for such a pattern within your own family charts? (For useful summaries of the conceptual literature on geographic migration see Lee 1966, and Tilly 1978.)

Fourth example – 'Job mobility'

The information in the family history chart on each person's 'first real job' and 'most typical occupation' can be used to produce a variety of tables of job mobility that follow the basic format of Table 3.4a below.[8]

A large variety of tables of occupational mobility can be derived using this basic format. Traditionally, sociological studies of occupational mobility have looked at the intergenerational mobility of males by comparing the job status of the father with that of his son (Miller 1998). Two tables of *male intergenerational job mobility* can be derived from the family history charts: (1) a comparison of

Table 3.4a *Occupational mobility, basic format*[1]

Origin	Destination:									
	I & II	IIIa	IIIb	IVa & b	IVc	V & VI	VIIa	VIIb	X	Total
I & II 'Service'										
IIIa Upper non-manual										
IIIb Routine non-manual										
IVa & b Proprietor										
IVc Farmer										
V & VI Skilled										
VIIa Semi- and unskld										
VIIb Agri worker										
X House-spouse										
Total										

[1] CASMIN Occupational Categories (adapted) (Erikson et al. 1988).

I & II	Professionals, upper-level managers and businessmen with significant numbers of employees
IIIa	Supervisors of non-manual employees and non-manual workers with significant skills or responsibilities
IIIb	Clerical workers, office workers, shop assistants
IVa & b	Proprietors of small (family) businesses
IVc	Farmers and farm managers
V & VI	Manual supervisors, foremen and skilled workers (requiring apprenticeship-level training)
VIIa	Semiskilled and unskilled manual workers
VIIb	Agricultural workers
X	Housespouses

the 'most typical' job of each man in the 'grandparent' generation with each of their sons in the 'parent' generation and (2) the same comparison, only between each man in the 'parent' generation and each of his sons in the 'target individual's' generation.

This traditional approach to the study of occupational mobility has been roundly criticized because it concentrates upon men only, in effect ignoring half of the population (see, for example, Dex 1990; McRae 1990; Payne and Abbott 1990; Hayes and Miller 1993; and Sorenson 1994). The balance can be redressed by producing tables of *female intergenerational job mobility* that are the equivalent to those for men, only making the comparison between the 'most typical' jobs held by mothers/grandmothers and their daughters (see Table 3.4b below).

However, such woman-only tables of occupational mobility have been criticized in turn for being unrealistic. Many women's 'most typical occupation' during their lifetime would have been that of 'housewife', particularly for the older generations. Coding 'origin' by the mother's job status may have the effect of masking the real social background, which will have been determined by the job a woman's father had. So, an alternative is to produce hybrid tables of intergenerational mobility in which the occupational status of the woman is compared with the occupational status of her father.

Finally, job mobility also takes place during people's own lifetimes. This is termed *intragenerational* or *career* mobility. Tables of intragenerational mobility can be produced for each generation in the family history chart by comparing each person's 'first real job' with their 'most typical occupation' during their lifetime.

This adds up to a large number of potential tables of occupational mobility, which are summarized in Table 3.4b.

Rather than generate all 12 tables, you or your class may decide to concentrate upon a subset of tables that is relevant to your interests. For instance, an interest in the social mobility of women would make the tables of female intergenerational mobility, 'hybrid' intergenerational mobility and female intragenerational mobility the most relevant.[9]

As a guide to interpreting occupational mobility tables generally, examine Table 3.4c below. The 'Total' column along the right-hand side depicts the distribution of the 'most typical occupation' of the mothers and the 'Total' row along the bottom depicts the occupa-

Table 3.4b   *Tables of occupational mobility*

Male intergenerational[1] mobility	Grandfathers by Fathers/uncles Fathers by sons
Female intergenerational[1] mobility	Grandmothers by Mother/aunts Mothers by daughters
'Hybrid' intergenerational[1] mobility	Grandfathers by Mother/aunts Fathers by daughters
Male intragenerational[2] mobility	Grandfather's generation Father's generation Son's generation
Female intragenerational[2] mobility	Grandmother's generation Mother's generation Daughter's generation

[1] Intergenerational mobility compares the 'most typical' occupations of a parent and their child.
[2] Intragenerational mobility compares a person's 'first real job' with their 'most typical occupation'.

tional distribution of the daughters. Comparing these two distributions can give an insight into changes in the occupational structure over time – what is termed 'structural mobility'. The main contrast between the mothers' and daughters' generations has been the drop in the proportion who spent the majority of their working lives in the home, from two-thirds (68 per cent) in the mothers' generation to one-third in the daughters' generation.

The diagonal of cells running from the upper left-hand corner of the table to the lower right-hand corner indicates 'inheritance' or, more accurately, those cases where the category of the daughter's occupation is the same as that of her mother. Note that almost all of the daughters who are presently housewives had mothers who also were housewives. The opposite, however, does not hold because of structural changes in the occupational distribution between the generations (the drop in the proportion of women remaining in the home and the consequent rise in women working in the outside economy). The shrinking proportion of women in housework means that many daughters whose mothers were housewives must themselves be active in the formal work economy.

Table 3.4c   *Female intergenerational occupational mobility, Malaysia*[1,2]

Mothers	Daughters									
	I & II	IIIa	IIIb	IVa & b	IVc	V & VI	VIIa	VIIb	X	Total
I & II 'Service'	–	–	–	–	–	–	–	–	–	–
IIIa Upper non-man	–	–	4%	–	–	–	–	–	–	1%
IIIb Routine non-man	6%	14%	11%	–	–	–	–	–	–	4%
IVa & b Proprietor	6%	29%	7%	44%	–	–	9%	–	6%	11%
IVc Farmer	–	–	4%	11%	100%	–	9%	–	–	4%
V & VI Skilled	–	–	–	–	–	–	–	–	–	–
VIIa Semi- and unskld	–	14%	–	–	–	33%	9%	–	–	3%
VIIb Agri worker	6%	14%	–	–	–	–	45%	–	–	10%
X House-spouse	82%	29%	75%	44%	–	67%	27%	–	94%	68%
Total	16%	6%	25%	8%	1%	3%	10%	–	32%	100%

[1] Percentages are based upon the educational distributions reported from the family history charts of 36 students at the Universiti Kebangsaan Malaysia, 1997.
[2] Except for the bottom 'Total' row, all percentages are column percentages, summing to 100% down each column.

Because the occupational categories tend to be ranked from 'highest' to 'lowest', the cells in the table above the diagonal, those on the upper right-hand side, basically indicate cases where people have been downwardly mobile and those on the lower left-hand side of the table below the diagonal indicate those who have been upwardly mobile. Note that almost all of the cells in the upper right-hand are empty; there has been little downward mobility.

These principles – comparing the 'marginal distributions' of the row totals with those of the column totals in order to gain insight into structural changes, noting that the cells along the diagonal indicate 'inheritance' or no change in status, and noting that the cells in the upper right-hand of the table indicate downward mobility while those in the lower left-hand indicate upward mobility – can be applied to mobility tables generally.

Combining results

The above tables generated from your family history chart will provide an indication of how historical and social changes have moulded the life experiences of people in your family over the last three generations. However, any extended family, even a very large one, can only show a limited picture of the parameters of a whole society. In order to provide a more encompassing perspective of the wider social currents that will have been affecting individuals over the previous decades, the tables generated by the whole class need to be collated together into a single set of 'master tables' in which all the data from each person's family is combined.[10] Once the set of collated tables are produced, they should be duplicated and brought to a class for a discussion that will centre around what the tables reveal about social phenomena and processes. During that discussion, the individual student will want to consider the extent to which his or her extended family is 'typical' of the general phenomena revealed in the tables.

The data in the collated tables cannot be considered to be truly representative in the sense of a properly conducted social survey. Since most students will have used their own families to construct the charts, most of the families contain at least one university student and hence the 'sample' of people collected in the families will be biased in favour of higher educational qualification. While people in the 'target individual's' generation will be younger than those in the 'parent' generation who in turn will be younger than those in the 'grandparent' generation, there will be considerable overlap in the age bands that make up the three generations. Some people will have selected a relatively young 'target individual' and if the people in the two preceding generations were young when they had their children, the whole span of the family history chart may cover only 60 years. On the other hand, if a person chose an older target individual who themselves was one of the youngest of their family generation and if the two preceding generations all continued to have children into their middle age, the time span of a family history chart can easily exceed a century. Finally, students who chose to chart a family which has had high fertility across all three generations will have a much larger number of individual 'cases' to contribute than someone who selected a family that has had a low rate of fertility across the three generations. If both sets of grandparents had large numbers of children (in previous generations in Northern Ireland, for example, families with ten or more children were not uncommon) and all of these survived and in turn produced large families, a family history chart with more than 200 individuals is easily possible (and more than 1,000 is theoretically possible!). At the other extreme, two generations of single-child families could produce a chart with only seven individuals (a very poor choice of a 'target individual'!).

Hence, the data contained in the collated tables cannot be considered to be statistically representative of the society from which it has been drawn. The goal of a family history study is to collect information that will be *illustrative* of those social processes that have affected families over a long span of time. If a statistically representative sample from which valid population parameters can be estimated is the desired goal, the correct solution is to carry out a probability based sample survey rather than conduct a family history study.

Nevertheless, even a small class of students will collect information on a surprisingly large number of individuals. While the numbers will vary widely, the 'typical' family history chart on average will have approximately 35 individuals. In a class of 25 students, this means information on 875 people – if not representative, at least a quite respectably sized sample! To code and process the individual data yielded by Social Genealogies *as if* they had come from a random sample of individuals would be to miss their main feature, which is [that they are] *relational'* (Bertaux 1995: 82). While the information in the tables should not considered as 'hard' data on social structure, significant features observed in the tables will correspond to significant phenomena that actually have occurred in the wider society. For instance, in a table of male intergenerational occupational mobility, the exact percentage distributions of jobs in the present and previous generations will not mirror the true population parameters. Nevertheless, the ways in which the distribution of jobs in the current generation have changed relative to the distribution of jobs in the previous generation *will* be reflected in the table. In that sense, the 'micro' data drawn from the family history charts can be considered to mirror the 'macro' features of the larger society.

The distributions for the 'previous' or 'parents' generation in a quantitative social mobility survey which is based upon a probability sample can also only be indicative of past distributions and cannot be statistically representative for any definite time in the past. This is due to differential fertility – parents who had many offspring are more likely to have had one of their children picked up in the present-day random sample than parents who had few children. Additionally information on people in the past who had no children or whose children have left the country or died early also will not be picked up by a present-day mobility sample. Interestingly, information about such people, who will be missed by a probability-based sample, *can* be picked up in a family history study. In such instances, the family history method is more truly representative than a probability survey (see the Methodological Note at the end of the chapter).

Exercise 3: In-depth interviews[11]

After making out the chart and constructing and analysing the tables, interview at least two relatives about how they view the 'history' of the family across the generations. In order to obtain a broad perspective on the family's history, interview one person from each of the older generations and one person of each sex.[12] The topics that are concentrated upon in the interviews will depend upon your own family's history and what you have noticed from the charts and tables. The following is a list of suggestions that may help produce insightful and interesting interviews:

1 Members of the older generations could be asked about how major historical events actually affected the family; for

example, events such as the Second World War, the depression of the 1930s and so on. Have there been lives lost in the family due to historical events? Note that the main effect upon a family of a major historical event can be migration. For example, the Great Depression in the United States led to the migration of the 'Oakies' to southern California and much post-World War II geographic mobility came from returning veterans whose horizons had been broadened by the places they had seen during the war. Similarly, students carrying out family history interviews in Northern Ireland regularly report relations who left the province due to the political violence. Sometimes this was because they were 'involved' and realized that the time had come to 'travel for their health', but more often they were the parents of male children who were approaching young adulthood (the prime age for both involvement in paramilitary activity and becoming a victim of the same) and wished to ensure the safety of their young male offspring. For families from a post-colonial nation, the gaining of the country's independence or a revolution can be a major watershed in the history of the family and the life chances of its members. The historical events that you choose to concentrate upon will depend upon the unique history of the geographic area or areas in which your family has been located over the last decades.

2 The effects of major social changes or trends can provide a fruitful line of inquiry for an interview; for example:
   - socio-economic changes, such as alterations in patterns of work (for example, the creation of more white-collar jobs), the replacement of apprenticeships by formal educational qualifications, the decline of small farming and so on;
   - the move to cities and other alterations in migration patterns;
   - changes in state social policy, such as the rise of the Welfare State with increased educational and health care provision – such changes may have dramatic effects such as greatly raising upward mobility or lowering the amount of child mortality;
   - demographic changes, such as drops in fertility or mortality across the three generations (and, if such changes have occurred, what are reasons for the changes?).

To put it another way, the topics and issues that you may have had in other social science courses can be applied here in order to provide a background for interviewing people in your family about their real experiences.

3   Since the interviews will span generations in the family, patterns of the transfer of material wealth between generations (inheritance) are a possible topic for interview. Perhaps because most students are relatively young and are not yet in the position to be a 'custodian' of family wealth, student family history interviews tend to turn up little about this important topic – when you do your interviews, consider probing for inheritance.

4   The effect of parents is almost bound to be significant. Note, however, that 'family effects' may cover more than just the link between parents and their offspring. Since the charts cover a wide collection of family members across several generations (and, as family structures become more complex through divorce [Riley 1986: 171–72]), try to assess whether there have been other important links or effects. For instance, investigate the possible role of aunts and uncles in affecting the social mobility of their nieces and nephews.[13]

5   Due to higher mortality in the past, it was not uncommon for marriages to be broken prematurely by the death of one spouse with the survivor remarrying and having additional children by their second spouse.[14] Paradoxically, today it is again becoming less uncommon for marriages to be broken prematurely – only now it is by divorce. In the future, the mid-twentieth century, when the norm was seen as stable nuclear families in which couples remained together until old age and brought up children within a unitary monogamous relationship, may come to be seen as an *abnormal* interlude between more complex family structures.

At every age there are increasing tendencies toward divorce and remarriage which contribute stepkin of varying ages to the family network. . . . The extent and configuration of the kinship structure have become so enlarged and complex (Unlenberg 1980), that traditional notions of family life stages no longer seem useful. Instead, I have come to view the kinship structure (Riley 1984) as a matrix of latent relationships – father with son, child with great-grandparent, sister with sister-in-law, ex-husband with ex-wife, and so on – a latent web of continually shifting linkages. These many diverse linkages provide new potentials for activating and intensifying close family relationships, and the options for close family bonds have multiplied. One can only imagine what these options may mean for future life stages of family members. (Riley 1986: 172–73)

If the most recent generation of your family seems to offer examples of such 'postmodern' family structures, the changing relationships brought by these altered structures may provide a topic for interview.

6 Try to establish 'the interactions between siblings' trajectories' (Bertaux 1995: 79). For instance, are there are birth order effects in your family? Elder siblings in work, for example, sometime contribute to the costs of keeping younger siblings in education. If an elder sibling is the first member of the family to attend college or university, often other members of the family may follow. Similar patterns can be seen for migration. Are there such patterns in your family?

7 By interviewing two people from previous generations, it may be possible to establish whether there have been changes in social relationships within the family over time. For example, did parents have more power in the past? Did relationships within the family in the past take the form of a patriarchy (or a matriarchy)? For example, previous family history exercises in Northern Ireland have found evidence for both patriarchal and matriarchal practices. Mothers tended more often to be the parent who decided whether a child would go further in education (or not). One area where sisters lost out in comparison to their brothers in past generations, however, was in staying in school. Many families seemed to have devoted their scarce resources to educating the boys at the expense of the girls (and almost a lifetime later this still can be bitterly resented by the women who were adversely affected). Many wives were reported as having the most influence in family decisions and control of day-to-day finances. However, few

women seemed to control family wealth or land as it was passed down. Women tend to be the people that maintain family links and act as repositories of information about the family; but does this signify power or a subservient position? And what about today? Could 'your' family be considered more egalitarian now, or does patriarchy or matriarchy persist?

Another possible avenue to explore would be changes in the extent and nature of contacts and support within the family. Was your family a true extended family in the past but is it now just a collection of related people? Traditionally, in an extended family the children worked in the family business and after marriage remained in the family home or very near by. If the members of a modern large family group live apart but keep in regular contact by telephone and provide significant support for each other, is this a modern adaptation of the old extended family form? From previous family history exercises in Northern Ireland, a consistent and interesting explanation for the prevalence of extended family contacts in the past was that these were not really just a feature of 'traditional' Irish society but rather *necessary* due to extreme poverty and the lack of state welfare provision. Families *had* to stick together in order to survive. This doesn't exactly contradict the standard sociological account, but it does differ from it in terms of emphasis.

8   Splits or divisions that have evolved in families over time can form the basis for a fruitful line of questioning. Has one whole branch of the family migrated to a new place or been socially mobile up to the middle class while the another branch has remained where it was? Lack of knowledge about a particular branch of the family, while a problem for completing the chart, may be an important clue to a family split. For instance, students in Northern Ireland occasionally have to report that they know almost nothing about a branch of their family. Quite often the explanation is that the link between the known and unknown branches of the family is a couple in a religiously mixed marriage. In these circumstances, religious sectarianism, family ostracism and social pressure sometimes can drive a wedge between the two parts of the family (see the Methodological Note at the end of the chapter).

9   Some families develop 'collective memories' – ways of view-
    ing the world in which the family is seen as playing a
    distinctive role within society. From a sociological standpoint,
    such family collective memories are 'considered to be the
    expression of a common family identity, transmitted from one
    generation to the next, acting as an anchoring-point for
    traditions and the maintenance of family characteristics.'
    (Muxel 1993: 193). As noted above, such collective memor-
    ies can be a feature of upper class families with a tradition of
    ruling (see also Lang 1998). Similarly, families that have
    remained in the same geographical location across many
    generations can develop a close affinity with the area. In
    Ireland, there are 'Republican' families – families with a strong
    nationalist tradition of political activism that covers genera-
    tions. A sign of such collective memories can be knowledge of
    'illustrious (or notorious) ancestors' or being able to trace the
    family genealogy back over many generations. You may want
    to direct your interviewing towards establishing the nature of
    'collective memories' within your own family: what are their
    content; how they are passed down and so on.

10 One of the most interesting things about family history
    research is how the explanations for changes across genera-
    tions have often been different from the received sociological
    myth. For instance, naïve sociology sees modern-day levels
    of increased educational attainment as an advancement
    which has promoted upward social mobility into white-collar
    work. Many of the accounts collected from older family
    interviewees in Northern Ireland, however, seemed to reverse
    the causal logic, implying that, in the past, decent (or at least
    as good as could be expected) jobs for young people were
    relatively easy to obtain (particularly for those moving into
    skilled manual work via apprenticeships), so there was no
    need to stay on in formal education. Nowadays, good jobs
    for young people are harder to find, so the only option is to
    stay on in education and hope that any qualifications
    obtained will help in getting decent work later on. Like less
    developed nations today, the idea of a large number of
    children as a form of insurance for one's old age was very
    prevalent in Western societies in the past. Accounts from

previous generations can imply that changing attitudes about the ideal number of children may be just as important as improved methods of contraception in explaining today's smaller family sizes. If you examine the older generation in your family history chart closely, you may note that the spacing of births is quite regular, and the number of children in the older generations, while larger than present-day families, in no way approaches the potential maximum fertility of a birth every year. Many families in the 'oldest' generation did seem to be quite capable of restricting fertility once the desired number of *surviving* children was attained.

11 Or whatever. The above are only suggestions. Each family will be unique and the circumstances of 'your' family may indicate a different, but no less fruitful, course of interview.

The following chapters on interviewing and the analysis of life histories provide guidelines that will help you conduct interviews with the members of 'your' family. After the interviews are complete, you should turn in a report which takes the form of an essay. The essay should be in two parts. Part 1 should be a fairly straightforward account of your family's 'history' based upon what you have noticed from your chart, the tables, and the interviews with your two family 'informants'; explaining who did what, why they did it, and any trends or patterns that you have noticed. The essay should take account of the issues of reliability and validity raised by the 'social dynamics' of the interviews (especially since many of you will be interviewing older members of your own family).

Then, for Part 2 of the essay, select a single sociological theme and try applying it to your family. Examples of an appropriate theme could be social mobility, the decline of the family, or any of the ideas which have been alluded to above or covered at some point in this course or in other relevant social science courses that you have taken. The purpose of this latter part of the essay is to give you a chance to *apply* the training in social science theories and concepts that you have received throughout your degree course. So, if you want to try out a sociological theme that *has not* been mentioned here, so much the better!

Appendix – Methodological Note

Family history charts for Northern Ireland tend to show a higher proportion of religiously mixed marriages than that which is usually given for the province. The explanation is that rather than facing the difficulties of maintaining a religiously mixed marriage in Northern Ireland ('difficulties' which can extend up to physical intimidation and violence), many mixed couples opt to leave the province altogether (Lee 1994). These out-migrants are then reported on the family history charts by their relations who have remained. This is another example of how the family history method can produce information that is more accurate than traditional surveys that are based on probability samples.

Bertaux (1995) has made similar observations:

> From the point of view of representativity Social Genealogies have an interesting property: through the inclusion of uncles and aunts into the window of observation, they allow us to reach out for the life trajectories of members of previous generations who did *not* have descendants, thus correcting a built-in bias of classical surveys on intergenerational social mobility, whose samples necessarily omit childless persons in the previous generations. This feature takes on added significance when childlessness is not a random phenomenon but a social historical one, concerning whole groups: witness, for example, in Québec [and Ireland], the key social-historical role of Catholic priests and nuns, who were long in charge not only of 'paroisses' but also of the education, health and even local government of the French-Catholic Canadians; or elsewhere, the generations decimated by war before they had the time to bear children; or those men and women who were the victims of harsh political repression in their young years; or the phenomenon of emigration, by which sizeable parts of a generation disappear from retrospective reconstructions based on samples of the next generation. In all these cases the construction of social genealogies allows us to restore the original place, existence, life trajectories and especially the influence of these men and women, provided that at least one of their kin remained within the population under observation and had children. (Bertaux 1995: 82)

Notes

[1] In any case, the idea that large multi-generational extended families were superseded by small, two-generation nuclear families during industrialization is itself an example of a sociological myth that collapses when subjected to empirical evaluation (such as the collection of family histories).

[2] One reason for a smaller number of children in the most recent, 'target individual's' generation may be that some people are still having children. This, however, should not be a factor for the two older generations which will have completed their child-bearing. Also, many people in the youngest generation probably will have no more children anyway.

[3] The practice of including all children who were born alive will have the effect of raising the fertility measure since not all of these children necessarily will survive to child-bearing age themselves. But, on the other hand, note that the older family members who are providing the information often have forgotten or chose not to mention babies who were born but died in infancy or early child-hood – particularly if these early deaths occurred a long time ago before the respondent's birth.

[4] Also polygamous marriages.

[5] The CASMIN schema of educational coding used in Table 3.2 was developed for purposes of international comparison by the research project Comparative Analysis of Social Mobility in Industrialized Nations. It has been utilized here because it can deal with variations between differing educational structures; that is, differences between societies or, of relevance for this exercise where different generations are being compared, differences in the educational system of a *single* society across a long period of time. It is presented here as a suggestion. All of the categories used may not apply to your location and your class may wish to discuss and agree suitable modifications to the schema of educational categories.

The interpretation of some of the categories may become clearer with some additional explanation:

- Most societies have a legal minimum amount of education which all children should receive. Despite this, many people obtain less schooling than the legal minimum. The first three categories are grouped around the amount of education that was the legal minimum during the individual's childhood. Note that for people of different ages, the legal minimum may be different as, for example, the school leaving age is raised over time.
- 'Vocational' refers to practical training that will be of direct relevance for a job;
- 'Maturity' is the amount of education that is required for entry into a university. In many societies 'maturity' is also a common endpoint for people's formal education.
- 'Postgraduate' refers to education beyond a first degree at the tertiary level.

If you require further information about the CASMIN categories, see König et al. (1987).

[6] The 'target individuals' chosen by these university students for their family history charts usually would have been one of their parents.

[7] This generation experienced very little movement to and from the south of Ireland, so the Republic of Ireland is not shown as a separate category in the table.

[8] The CASMIN schema of occupational coding used in Tables 3.4a and 3.4c was developed for purposes of international comparison by the research project Comparative Analysis of Social Mobility in Industrialized Nations. The schema has been utilized here because, as with the CASMIN educational coding, it can deal with variations between societies or within a *single* society across a long period of time.

[9] In fact, the number of 'social mobility' tables that could be generated from the family history chart is much greater than 12. Tables of intergenerational *educational* mobility could be produced by comparing the CASMIN educational codings of parents with those of their children. Also, the effect of education upon the later worklife could be investigated by producing tables of people's educational attainment by their 'first real job' and/or their 'most typical occupation' to see the extent to which higher educational attainments have been converted into higher status jobs. Which tables are generated is a matter of choice, with the choice being determined by the research interests of you and your group. (Since the focus of this chapter is especially upon families as they are affected by social change across several generations, the most fruitful comparisons to make may be the six tables to do with intergenerational occupational mobility.)

[10] While a fairly mechanical process, this combination of data does require careful organization. The tables will need to be brought together for the person or persons who has undertaken to collate them. That person will need sufficient time to calculate the resulting percentages and produce copies for distribution to the whole group. This task is too involved to be done on an *ad hoc* basis during classtime.

[11] The next chapter will be about conducting life history interviews and will have in-depth interviewing exercises at its end which could be combined with this interviewing exercise. The development of family history charts and the taking of life history interviews can be linked. Issues arising from the examination of your family history chart and the quantitative tables derived from it can act as background for an in-depth life history interview or interviews.

[12] This is an ideal that may not attainable. While a spread across the generations and sexes is desirable, it may not always be possible. People may not be available for interview or simply refuse. Also, especially with the oldest generation, there may not be any surviving members capable of giving a coherent and lengthy interview.

[13] On a personal note, I have one uncle who lived abroad throughout his whole working life and another who was a prominent university

professor – these facts have more than a coincidental relationship to my current situation, an expatriate American working in a university in Northern Ireland.

[14] In extreme cases where both husband and wife died in turn, the older children in a large family could find themselves living in a unit in which neither of their 'parents' were their natural parents.

4

Collecting Life Histories

CONTENTS

Whether I shall turn out to be the hero of my own life, or whether that station will be held by anybody else, these pages must show. To begin my life with the beginning of my life, I record that I was born (as I have been informed and believe) on a Friday, at twelve o'clock at night. It was remarked that the clock began to strike, and I began to cry, simultaneously. . . .

The first paragraph of *David Copperfield* by Charles Dickens

As established in Chapter 1, the collection of life histories or life stories and their related 'cousin', family histories, have been methods of research that have grown remarkably in popularity over recent decades. Their popularity has waxed across a variety of social science disciplines – sociology, social policy, political science, anthropology and social psychology to name a few. As well as being distinct methods of research, they also have come to be seen as embodying a distinct approach to social science – the biographical perspective. This perspective is located soundly, within the general 'qualitative paradigm' of social science research but has distinct characteristics. In particular, a holistic concern with placement in time, the interplay between the individual actor and social structure and how this interplay and its perception alters with the passage of time. This chapter will turn to the practical considerations of adopting the biographical perspectives; in particular, to the consideration of issues that surround the collection of biographical data.

When to collect life histories?

The biographical perspective should not be seen as a universal panacea or a method of research that is always superior to other techniques. There are particular circumstances under which a biographical approach is indicated and these circumstances are intimately related to the foci of the perspective. The biographical perspective is *holistic*. This holistic viewpoint expresses itself in two ways.

Firstly, biographical data range across time. The respondent who is telling us about their biography or family history does so in the present, but this biography or family history ranges over the past. The typical life history will cover the events of the respondent's life course up to the present. Hence, a biographical approach is indicated where the area of interest is either the effects of change across time, historical events as these events have impinged upon the individual, or his or her movement along their life course. The techniques of biographical interviewing (as discussed below) facilitate recall through a process of cross-referentiality as the respondent moves back and forth in their life history and makes linkages between different types of events and segments of their life.

EXAMPLE: As mentioned in the Preface, in order to provide material to illustrate the various approaches to biographical research, a series of life history interviews have been carried out with 'William', a middle-aged professional married man living in Belfast, Northern Ireland. A very important part of William's life is his involvement in athletics and running. Here, within an account of athletics events and a sports club that he has been instrumental in setting up, William makes a number of cross-references to other aspects of his life: to his first house purchase; his marriage; and his career. Note how William uses his age and the definite dates of the establishment of the club and his marriage to set the events in a time frame:

> [Organizing events and developing the club] has involved me for a number of years at, eh, back in the late, I suppose, the mid to late . . . 70s. . . . I was about 27, 28. I bought a house . . . a little semi-detached house . . . in _____ just off 'Parkview' Road . . . with Belfast Running Club open in 1977. It was extremely convenient when I wanted to go down for a drink. I just had to walk down there. And I met my wife through athletics [at the club]. She doesn't run herself. Eh, as I say, we got married in 85. . . . and so when [cough] when I got married, it was an unusual situation. My wife, who lived in this area I just had described, _____, I'm sure you can find another name for it [laugh] . . . I moved into my wife's house. It was bigger and had more scope, and certainly, one of the rooms lent itself as an, eh, as an office. [This was the point in his career when William left the public sector and made the risky move into private practice.]

In the hands of a skilled interviewer, cross-referentiality could even be extended to the point that at least partially reliable information on the previous psychological states of an individual may be gleaned.[1]

Secondly, the biographical perspective centres itself midway between social structure and the individual as social actor. To tell about one's biography means telling about the constraints and opportunities that were available in the past and how one dealt with these – circumventing (or being thwarted by) obstacles, taking advantage of (or missing) opportunities. The biographical perspective is about the interplay between actor and social structure – how the individual has negotiated their path through a changing societal structure.[2]

Unless the respondent is very old and sees himself/herself at the end of their life, any biographical account, as well as the life it purports to represent, will be presented as incomplete. The respondent will have plans and hopes for the future. The strategic nature of this account expands the time span of the biographical perspective from the past *through* the present into the future. In telling their 'life story' most people will assume that 'the final chapters' remain to be written, as it were. The account that a respondent is giving of their past life can be coloured by their anticipation of the directions their life may take in the future.[3] Hence, the biographical perspective is particularly appropriate when a viewpoint is required that is aware of the context of changing social structure and the passage of time.

Negotiating with respondents

Before interviewing commences, there are a number of issues that the researcher must resolve. These include sampling; finding cases; arranging interviews; and reaching a 'contract'.

Sampling

Locating suitable respondents for study is a problem that first-time biographical researchers often fail to appreciate at the outset. Biographical research is qualitative research and the standard quantitative method of drawing a probability sample randomly from a population will not (usually!) produce suitable candidates. Other means of selection are required.

One method of selection is 'happenstance'. This is not as flippant as it sounds. Through chance circumstances the researcher may become aware of an individual or group that provide an opportunity for a valid research project. For instance, the landmark study of 'Jane Fry', a transvestite, by Bogdan and Taylor apparently came about due to a chance encounter (Plummer 1983). One cannot set out to stumble across an individual or group that would make an ideal research study, but much can be gained from having the presence of mind to recognize a good opportunity for research if it should arise.[4]

One however cannot always trust to chance to provide research projects! The usual procedure for selecting respondents for biographical research is that of selective sampling (Schatzman and Strauss 1973). Selective sampling differs from the techniques of probability sampling that are used by survey researchers. In selective sampling, the people used in the study are chosen on a conceptual basis.[5] Comparatively small numbers are selected and each person has been chosen because they

are deemed to represent a certain type or group that is considered *on conceptual grounds* to be important. The goal of the
sampling is to secure a spread of individuals that represent all
of the types or groups that are significant for the phenomenon
or topic under consideration. The classic study of artisanal
bakers in France conducted by Bertaux and Bertaux-Wiame
provides an example of the use of selective sampling within the
realist approach (Bertaux and Bertaux-Wiame 1981a and 1981b).
Bertaux and Bertaux-Wiame were interested in the question of
how the French bread-baking industry had maintained a tradition of small, private bakers when most other industrialized
nations had switched to large-scale factory-produced bread.

Respondents were chosen by virtue of fitting into the category
of small-time baker (or the spouse of a baker). The only refinement to this sampling strategy was a subsequent division into
master bakers, who had succeeded in procuring their own shops,
and employees, who worked for other bakers. This latter sub-
division was driven by the results of analysis. Bakers were
chosen for interview until Bertaux and Bertaux-Wiame realized
that 'saturation' had been reached – the point at which new interviews failed to provide additional information but merely reit-
erated previously noted patterns (less than 100 cases).[6] From a
qualitative viewpoint, this selection of bakers met the criteria of
both representativeness and generalizability. The division into
master and journeymen bakers covered the two significant categories for analysis and hence the sample can be considered representative of bakers. The attainment of 'saturation' meant that
new interviews would not add significantly to what had been
found already, so the existing sample was all that was required in
order to generalize to bakers and bakery workers as a whole.

Selective sampling differs radically from probability sampling as used in quantitative research. In probability sampling,
a number of cases are chosen by a random chance procedure
from a general population that ideally includes all the possible
elements of interest. The number randomly chosen is large
enough so there is a high probability that the characteristics of
the sample mirror those of the whole population within a small
margin of error. This reliable mirroring means that the sample is
deemed to be representative – one can generalize from the
sample to the whole population in that any relationships

observed in the sample should also exist in the whole population. While the goal of each sampling procedure is the same – to
gain knowledge about the whole population (in this case, all
bakers) – the rationale underlying the sampling procedures
differs widely. The numbers chosen in a selective sample will be
much smaller – once an adequate number of cases (as judged by
the researcher) have been chosen to represent all of the main
variety of phenomena in the groups of interest, there is no need
to take any more. Selective sampling is based upon deliberately
choosing individuals who typify certain conceptually based
types, the proportions chosen need not match their overall
prevalence in the general population. Probability sampling is
based upon selecting individual elements without any regard to
any characteristic except their inclusion within the definition of
the population.[7]

Biographical researchers following the neo-positivist approach
also use selective sampling-type procedures to choose their
cases. Working from theory to data, a neo-positivist biographical
researcher would be even more tightly bound by conceptual
criteria than the realist in his/her selection of cases.

As discussed in the introductory chapter and below, the third
approach to biographical research, the narrative approach, is
distinguished from the other two by its view of the nature of
interview/interviewee interaction and its vision of the reality
that biographical research can elicit. This has important consequences for the manner in which an interview is conducted
and for the subsequent analysis, but the starting point for a
narrative researcher can be that of either grounded theory or
theory-testing. This means that the strategies for selecting cases
for a Narrativist will also be those followed by Realists or neo-
Positivists.

Finding cases

Researchers using selective sampling will be seeking respondents who fall into the categories relevant to their study. If the
'types' being sought are relatively numerous or concentrated in
certain areas or within certain organizations, such as Bertaux
and Bertaux-Wiame's bakers, locating suitable candidates may
be fairly easy.[8] Finding cases, however, is not always straightforward. Biographical research has had a long-standing associa-

tion with the sociology of deviance. It may be that the groups of interest are engaged in illegal or illicit activities that make locating them difficult or dangerous. Neo-Positivists may be employing focused conceptual criteria in their theoretical sampling that means they seek groups that, while they exist, may be hard to identify. Such considerations mean that the researcher often has to go to great lengths to locate cases for research. The problem that the researcher faces is similar to that of a market research interviewer who has been given a quota sample by their firm. The market research interviewer has to find people who match a predetermined set of characteristics, a 'quota'. Interviewers learn to exercise their ingenuity to locate people who match their quotas – going to a local train or bus stop to find users of public transport, 'working' the streets near a university to find young educated adults in their early 20s, going to a bingo hall to find retirees, and so on. A biographical researcher with a self-imposed set of quotas set by the demands of a selective sample will need to exercise the same level of ingenuity.

There are additional strategies that some researchers have used with success. Advertising can be a way of getting suitable candidates to come forward. The original *pamictniki* (written autobiographies) were solicited by newspaper advertisement. The same method has been used in contemporary studies; for example, Kontula and Haavio-Mannila (1995) used newspaper advertisements to procure written 'sexual life histories' from the general public.

'Snowball sampling' can be a means of procuring interviews with a group that is rare or hard-to-find (perhaps due to being proscribed or engaging in illegal activities) but nevertheless constitutes a network of contacts. If the researcher gains the confidence of an initial respondent, the original subject may then be willing to pass the interviewer on to a second 'contact' or member of the network, who in turn does the same for a third, and so on.

Large-scale quantitative survey research can be combined with the collection of life histories. This is particularly useful for neo-positivist biographical researchers who want to centre their life history interviews on respondents whose selection has been closely defined by pre-existing conceptual criteria. The author was involved in such a study. The study, of gender and political participation in Northern Ireland, began with the large-scale sample survey of 1,600 respondents drawn randomly from the whole population. A central premise of the project was that the usual indices of political participation were biased in favour of the types of political activity indulged in by men and hence underestimated the true level of women's political activity. The first stage of the study was a survey interview schedule that incorporated extensive measures of political participation, many of which had been developed by the investigators, that were set up to give equal weight to types of activities, such as community level politics, that women could be expected to be involved in. On the basis of their answers to the survey, each respondent was given a 'score' for their level of political activity. Those respondents scoring the highest were then contacted for a second, qualitative reinterview that included the taking of a 'political life history' – how they came to be politically active. The questions on the interview schedule that were used to develop the indices of political activity were careful operationalizations of theories about types and parameters of political participation. The people who were found to score high on these indices of political participation were then chosen for reinterview with their selection being determined not on grounds of statistical representativeness but rather solely by their level of activity. Hence, the second, life history, stage of the project was a sample based upon conceptually derived criteria. Note that, without the results from the first stage quantitative survey, it would have been impossible to carry out the theoretical sampling for the second stage of biographical interviewing. (For a complete account of the study and its results, see Miller et al., 1996.)

Arranging interviews

Whatever procedure is used to contact participants in a biographical study, the next task will be to secure the co-operation of the potential respondents. Do not expect enthusiastic agreement. Collecting a life history, even one focused on only a limited part of the life or limited only to certain topics, is bound to be a lengthy process. At a minimum, you should anticipate an interview lasting several hours. The open-ended nature of asking someone to 'tell about their life' means that the time devoted to an interview can run on indefinitely. Life history

interviewing can mean more than one interview with a respondent and intensive life history interviews with a single respondent
have been known to stretch over many sessions scattered over
years. You must give a reasonable estimate to a potential
respondent of the time you anticipate the interviewing will
take. You should do this for both ethical and practical reasons.
One should not deliberately mislead a potential respondent
about the amount of time they may have to give for an
interview. In any case, if you give a gross underestimate, the
potential interviewee may realize that you are misleading them
and either refuse to consent to an interview or terminate the
process early if it is running over time. Some people may
simply be unwilling or unable to commit the time.

Secondly, to put it bluntly, taking a life history interview is an
invasion of privacy. You are asking someone to tell you everything of note about all or some aspect of their life. Again, this is
an open-ended commitment that people may not feel capable of
meeting. 'Skeletons in closets', real or imagined, do exist and
people may not care to reveal these to a stranger, even if that
stranger has wrapped himself/herself in a cloak of academic
neutrality. (If the potential respondent and interviewer already
are known to each other the problem is only exacerbated.)

Finally, some people who are approached about telling their
life histories may have misgivings about the effects upon their
own psychological stability if they put themselves through
the experience. Enthusiastic life history researchers sometimes
naïvely assume that telling one's life history must be a therapeutic experience. This is not necessarily the case. Telling one's
own life story is bound to be an exercise in introspection. If a
potential respondent has misgivings about whether this exercise is advisable for them, these misgivings quite probably have
a genuine basis and should be respected.[9]

Reaching a 'contract'

Assuming that you are successful in locating a participant
willing to give you their life history, it is advisable to agree a
'contract' prior to commencing the interviews. This does not
mean that a formal, witnessed document should be drawn up
and signed (though some North American researchers (for example, Atkinson, 1998) advocate just such a formal procedure),

but rather that clear ground rules for the interview and the use of the information arising from it should be agreed explicitly beforehand.

It is in your own interest as researcher to secure a commitment from your respondent that they will 'stay the course'; that is, carry out a complete interview or sequence of interviews and not withdraw their permission for you to use the information coming from their life story. It could be disastrous for your research if a respondent quit half-way through an interview series or, even worse, demanded at a some later date that their material be expunged from any analysis or publication.

The commitment from the respondent should be an 'informed commitment'; they should have a clear idea as to the amount of time they will be devoting to the interviews and about the uses to which their material will be put in analysis and publication. Remember that the respondent may not understand all of the implications of what they have agreed to at the outset and it is up to you to make these clear.

Establish at the beginning whether there will be any 'off limits' topics. If controversial topics or the collection of intimate details are likely to make up part of the interview, this should be made known at an early stage in the research. The respondent should know that if the interview does enter an unanticipated area that makes them uncomfortable, they can declare their discomfort without losing face. You may want to save the asking of 'difficult' questions to a later stage in the interview, with a clear break point. A partial interview can be better than no interview at all. Also, by the latter stages of an interview, sufficient rapport may have been established with the respondent, or they may feel, having invested considerable time and effort into the interview, that they are willing to accept lines of questioning that would have been ruled out at the beginning.[10]

Some respondents may not mind the possibility of being identified (or even relish it!), but most would feel uncomfortable with exposing one's personal life details to strangers. Before commencing with interviewing, you should establish whether the respondent's identity will remain confidential, and the extent to which confidentiality genuinely can be maintained. The collection and publication of a life history by its nature means that a large amount of personal detail about single individuals will be placed in the public domain. The use of pseudonyms and the obscuring or alteration of details that are peripheral to the research may be all that is required to maintain full confidentiality (Atkinson 1998: 37–38). If the interviewee is well-known or part of a small group or if the demands of the research are such that some essential details cannot be masked that could allow for the person to be identified, however, it may be that an assurance of full confidentiality cannot be given.

EXAMPLE: William works in a profession followed by a relatively small number of people who would be well-known to each other in Belfast. Furthermore, he is extremely active in a minority sport and generally has a high profile of public service activity. In order to maintain William's confidentiality, it was necessary to alter quite a lot of his personal details; in particular to change his profession and substitute another minority sport that is organized along lines similar to his real avocation. The solution was to discuss with William which profession and sport could be substituted for the real ones while still retaining the distinctive characteristics of his patterns of work (a profession that requires a period of placement after obtaining a degree before full accreditation is reached) and sporting involvement (an organized sport linked to a university background and an upper middle-class lifestyle but also a sport that, unlike rugby or golf, is a minority interest).

Confidentiality, and the lengths to which a researcher is prepared to go to maintain it, becomes a particularly salient issue if respondents are involved in illegal or politically sensitive acts. The researcher needs to decide beforehand the amount of official coercion they are willing to resist. To put it baldly, are you willing to face criminal proceedings yourself in order to protect a respondent?[11]

Another important issue to clear up prior to interviewing is the degree of control that the respondent will have over the final results. This ranges along a continuum from no control or involvement by the respondent after the interviewing is over, to including the interviewee as a joint co-author:

1 No control. The respondent has no sight of interview transcripts or any control over the publication of results, including *verbatim* quotes from their interviews. The end of interviewing is the conclusion of all contact between the interviewer and interviewee; if the respondent sees published results that include his/her material, this happens only due to chance or through their own initiative. It is worth noting that this extreme end of the continuum may well be the most typical type of research relationship, perhaps outnumbering all of the other alternatives that follow. The 'one-sidedness' of the arrangement does raise ethical issues about whether the research relationship is exploitative, but an ethical defence can be made (see below). Outside of raising ethical questions, narrativists in particular would argue strongly that excluding the respondent totally from any involvement in the process of analysis also is questionable on methodological grounds.

2 Sight and comment on transcript accuracy.   Instead of terminating the research relationship at the end of the last interview, the researcher can give the respondent the opportunity to read and comment upon the accuracy of transcripts of their interviews. This can increase accuracy if the transcripts are summaries or paraphrases rather than straight word-for-word transcriptions. Improving literal accuracy is less well served if the transcriptions are *verbatim* texts, but this procedure still has advantages.[12] Allowing the respondent to go over the transcripts in effect constitutes an additional interview – giving the respondent the chance to expand upon points that they with hindsight see as requiring additional explanation. (Though the downside is that they may wish to remove material that they now see as revealing too much.)

3 Sight and comment on interpretation.   The respondent can be brought further into the analytic process by showing them the results of analyses and interpretations that have been made of their interviews. At this point, one is 'crossing a line' as it were, and bringing the subject into the research as an active participant in analysis. This level of involvement, which could be seen as a practice that fits well with the narrative approach to biographical research, does raise ethical issues as well because it is considerably more invasive than simply carrying out an interview.

4 Sight and comment on publication.   Respondents can be given the opportunity to see and comment upon research findings that are slated for publication. This raises a number of issues. Are the respondent's rights over the publication limited to sight and comment, or do they have some sort of control over the content of what is eventually published? Is this control limited to being able to insert their own comments or reactions, a 'minority report', or are they given a veto over material appearing? If they do have a veto, is the right to exclude material limited to that attributable directly to them, especially direct quotes, or can it extend to excluding any findings or conclusions that may have resulted from the analysis of material they provided?[13] Is the respondent's involvement such that they should receive at least some of the credit for the research? Should they be listed as an author? And, if so, should they receive a share of any publication royalties? All of these questions become more pertinent when a study is dependent upon the intensive interview of a single case or when a respondent takes an active role in the process of interpretation and analysis to the extent that they can be considered a collaborator in the research.

Interviewing

Practical points

Having 'negotiated' an interview contract, one needs to carry out the interviews themselves. There are a number of practical considerations which must be taken into account if the interviews are going to go smoothly, such as costs, time and place, taping and transcription. Their neglect could spoil the success of the whole enterprise.

Costs Make accurate assessments of the costs of your data collection before you set out. While the expenses of qualitative research pale in comparison to the cost of a massive interview survey with a large sample, they nevertheless can be considerable – especially for students that may be absorbing all or part of the costs themselves. The researcher must travel to the interview or be prepared to meet the expenses of the respondents' travel. Travel can include having to find overnight accommodation. The interviews are almost surely going to be recorded, so the cost of tapes and possibly a good-quality tape machine will have to be met. If professional typists are being hired to produce transcripts of the interviews, they will have to be paid. Special equipment to help speed up the transcription process exists (such as headphones, and pedal controls with an automatic reverse whenever the tape is paused), but it costs money.

One should note that 'costs' means more than just money. Qualitative research places high demands upon the researcher's time. Interviews can be prolonged. As well as the time actually spent doing the interview, there may be a lengthy preparation phase. A researcher following the neo-positivist approach will need to devise questions and strategies that elicit information on the topics of interest without at the same time injecting a bias into the interviewee's responses. If multiple interviews with the same respondent are being done, the transcripts of the first interviews need to be reviewed prior to the subsequent interviews. A narrativist may elect to show the respondent transcripts from their earlier interviews or discuss preliminary findings based upon earlier interviews. All this will require careful preparation in advance.

Time and place Once a respondent has agreed to be interviewed, a time and place for the interview must be established. This will need to be at the convenience of the interviewee but there are considerations which you should push for. Try for a quiet location where the interview will not be disturbed and where the respondent will feel at ease. Avoid bars and coffee shops unless they are quiet ones. If the site of the interview is the respondent's home or office, try to ensure that you will not be disturbed during the interview. Being interrupted by telephone calls often are the worst problem – try to arrange for a member of the respondent's family or an office colleague to field them during the interview.

Avoid placing the interview under a time constraint. Allow for the maximum time you think the interview could possibly take, and then add on a bit. A really successful interview may well turn into a long one and nothing will spoil a productive discourse more effectively than having to hurry it in order to meet a deadline.

Taping You will want to tape record the interview if at all possible. A full *verbatim* account is almost a requirement for narrative-style research where the focus of analysis will be upon the interplay between interviewer and interviewee. The same holds for early realist interviews until saturation – the establishment of clear and regular patterns of response – is approached. The researcher is developing conceptual categories during the early stages of grounded theory-style realist interviewing and any system of note-taking will evolve dramatically over the first interviews. No matter which approach is followed, a tape recording of the whole interview provides an invaluable back-up for any system of note-taking.

The interviewee will need to be told in advance that you want to tape your conversation. They may need reassurance and should be given a truthful explanation of why taping is essential. On the day, most respondents quickly lose their inhibitions about being taped and forget the machine is there.

Some texts advocate leaving the tape recorder running after the 'official' interview is concluded. The assumption is that the respondent may relax and then make some 'off the cuff' remarks that can prove insightful. Do not try this. Firstly, deliberately tricking a person who has given an interview under good faith is questionable on ethical grounds. Secondly, people are not stupid and may see through your ploy. While they may have been relaxed about the tape recorder during the main interview, they can become acutely aware that it is still recording after you have told them the interview is over. Thirdly, the act of switching off the tape recorder does provide a little 'ritual' that gives the interview a clear terminal point. If the respondent then relaxes and does say something that is worth remembering, simply tell them that that is interesting and ask if you may make a note of it.

Though this may sound obvious, check the functioning of your tape recorder in advance. Familiarize yourself with the operation of its controls beforehand and do a test run to make sure the microphone is picking up sound clearly. If you will be using special transcription equipment, make sure tapes recorded on your recorder are compatible with it. Bring extra batteries and tapes. Take some care with the placement of the tape microphone so that it can pick up both your voice and the respondent's. Avoid putting the tape recorder on a hard surface such as a low table where the noise of knocks or kicks can obscure the conversation. The recorder should be placed where you can look over occasionally to see that the cassette is turning. Watch out for background noise that washes out conversation. Keep track of the time so that you are ready to start a new tape when the end of a cassette is reached. Finally, label tapes clearly immediately after an interview has been completed.

Transcription   The transcription of interviews is a lengthy process. If one is paying to have their interviews transcribed, the expense can be considerable. The person doing the transcription will need clear instructions about any conventions that need to be followed during the typing up of interviews.[14] (See Appendix 2 for a simple set of suggested conventions for transcription.) If you elect (or are forced by the expense) to do the transcription yourself, note that it will take at least three times as long to transcribe a tape as it took to carry out the interview.

In spite of the cost in time and money of transcription, you should attempt a full *verbatim* transcription of the complete interview if at all possible. Forcing an interview into a note or summarized form at the outset is, in effect, imposing an analytical structure on the information at a very early and probably premature stage. The chances of finding contrary evidence – realizing that your findings in fact fall into patterns different from those expected at the outset – are much reduced if the first analysis must begin from predigested notes.

Interviewing – General points[15]

The ability to carry out an effective interview is not something that is conferred automatically. Becoming a good interviewer is a skill that can be learned, but it requires practice. A good interview, particularly an interview conducted within the narrative approach or an unfocused initial interview, may resemble a casual conversation but one must remember that the format of the interview really is mimicking a conversation. There are constraints present in even the most unstructured interview. The topic of the conversation has a goal, albeit this goal may be the very general one of hearing the story of a person's life as they care to tell it. The two protagonists are likely to be strangers to each other. While the 'standard' prohibitions against the interviewer injecting their own feelings or opinions into the conversation may be relaxed in some styles of narrative interviewing, the focus of the interview will remain fixed upon the interviewee. These considerations lead to some general points that can be made about conducting life history interviews.[16]

The interviewer must not succumb to the temptation to hijack the interview as a platform for their own ideas. You should not argue with the respondent, attempt to convert them to your own opinions or monopolize the interview with your own life story or assertions. To put it baldly, the interview is not about the interviewer. If you come to dominate the interview so that the majority of the information is in fact about you or your own opinions, the interview will be useless. If you succeed in browbeating the interviewee so that he/she is silenced or gives way to your opinions, the information you are collecting will be positively misleading (Thompson 1988).

One can of course tactfully query or express disagreement with some of the respondent's opinions or assertions (either by saying that 'some people' might feel differently or, in some styles of interviewing, disagreeing yourself). The goals of these challenges to the interviewee's stance are not, however, to change their position or force them to adopt the 'right' (that is, *your*) viewpoint, but rather to clarify anomalies or to advance the interview. For instance, if the respondent is putting forth an opinion that many would disagree with, pointing this out can be a legitimate means of taking the interview further, but brow-beating them into abandoning their views is not. As Thompson points out, the key point is respect for the interviewee: 'There are some essential qualities which the successful interviewer must possess: an interest and respect for people as individuals, and flexibility in response to them; an ability to show understanding and sympathy for their point of view; and, above all, a willingness to sit quietly and listen' (Thompson 1988: 196).

Some general rules to keep in mind when interviewing:

1 Ask questions in everyday language and avoid complex wording. As well as being likely to confuse the respondent, the use of technical terms or jargon in effect is imposing your own viewpoint onto the respondent and forcing them to answer on your terms only.

2 The usual strictures against poorly worded questions that apply to formal questionnaire-type interviews also apply to

qualitative interviewing. You should avoid questions that are double negatives or implicit double negatives. (For example, *Please explain why you cannot stop drinking.*) Similarly, 'double-barrelled' (asking two separate questions at once) or leading questions should be avoided. Some years ago, the BBC in Northern Ireland commissioned a senior British political scientist to carry out a survey on political opinion in the province. The following question drawn from that survey manages to combine both types of error: '*Most people* think power sharing may be necessary for *ᵃpeace* and a *ᵇworkable local Parliament* in Northern Ireland, do you agree?' The question was deliberately designed to 'discover' a groundswell of support for a political solution in Northern Ireland. The phrase *Most people* was leading because for a person to disagree they would have to place themselves in the unreasonable 'minority' who disagreed. The question was double-barrelled because a person who agreed could either believe that *power sharing* was necessary for *peace* or for *a workable local Parliament* or for both.

Respondents of course can resist poor questioning. Note how William resists a leading question from the interviewer; the topic being covered was William's movement from job to job in his career in the public sector:

> *Interviewer*: And the contacts from each job sort of lead into the other one because they all were similar work?
> *William*: Well, similar work to a certain extent. The only other thing too they had in common . . . they all shared the same pension scheme [*an explanation of the pension scheme follows*].

3 If there are delicate questions that will be asked – say about private or personal matters or about politics – have versions of these ready beforehand and be prepared to ask them without hesitation or embarrassment.
4 'Probe generalizations; for example, "What was so good about school?" or "Could you describe some specific incidents?" ' (Wilton 1998: 27).
5 When respondents are giving long discursive replies, be willing to listen to the whole account even if they seem to be drifting off the point of the interview. 'Whenever possible avoid interrupting a story. If you stop a story because you

think it is irrelevant [you may be wrong and furthermore], you will cut off not just that one, but a whole series of subsequent offers of information which *will* be relevant. . . . Return to the original point at the end of the digression if you wish, with a phrase like "Earlier you were saying . . .", "Going back to . . .", or "Before we move on . . ." ' (Thompson 1988: 203 and 210).

6   The opposite also can be welcomed. Do not fear pauses. These can give a respondent the chance to gather their thoughts.

7   You must be prepared to concentrate during an interview and to follow your interviewee's train of thought (Wilton 1998: 27). When a semi-structured interview schedule is being used, you need to know which items have not yet been covered by the interviewee (particularly difficult if they are jumping from topic to topic). You do not want to make the blunder of asking about something they have told you about already.

8   'At the same time you should be watching for the consistency of the answers. . . . If you are doubtful about something, try returning to it from another angle, or suggesting, tactfully and gently, that there may be a different view of the matter – "I have heard" or "I have read that . . ." ' (Thompson 1988: 210).

9   Many researchers will make some notes during the interview even if they are taping. Notes can be a 'fail safe' – providing at least some backup if something goes wrong with the taping. You may want to take note of especially important points or give yourself reminders for later questions or for the analysis. An audio tape cannot record the non-verbal behaviour of the respondent. Body language such as changes in posture, frowns and so on may be giving valuable cues about their state of mind. If you are taking notes, explain to the respondent why you are doing so. If you have had to adopt a procedure where notes are made after an interview, make these notes as quickly as possible after the conclusion of the interview.

10   Finally, try to end the interview on an upbeat. 'An interview which ends on a relaxed note is more likely to be remembered as pleasant, and lead on to another' (Thompson 1988: 211).

Interviewing – Realist approach

The different approaches to the biographical perspective lead to distinctive styles of interviewing. The realist approach in its pure form employs a grounded theory mode of interviewing. The initial realist interview can be characterized as extremely unfocused. The interviewer says little – giving a brief introduction to the interviewee, only enough to get them started.[17] During the course of the first interview, the interviewer tries to remain as non-directive as possible.

EXAMPLE: Direct quotation from what was said to William at the start of his first interview may be illustrative.

> *Interviewer*: . . . tell me your life history or the story of your life. . . .
> I will say very little, and if I ask you any questions it will be
> mainly about something not clear to me, if I don't understand
> something. . . . So, just you take it in any order you want, if you
> want to start at your birth and work your way up, or work your
> way back, or take it thing by thing, it is up to you.[18]

Most of the interviewer's comments will be merely nods, vague assenting noises or encouragement to say more. Some interviewees with a little prompting prove themselves quite capable of a long and informative monologue, but this will not always be the case. If/As the interviewee begins to dry up, one non-directive strategy that sometimes works is to parrot back the respondent's last statement. For example:

> *Respondent*: That was the hardest thing I ever did . . . not going
> home that Christmas. [*Lengthy pause*]
> *Interviewer*: That was hard, not going home then. . . .

If an interview following this non-directive format goes on for some time, the interviewee can become quite hyper-sensitive to implicit direction in questions. One must remember that being subjected to a social science interview at length is an unusual experience. The closest parallels in everyday life would be situations in which a person is being evaluated, such as a job interview or an oral examination. Even when one makes the standard assurances that 'There are no wrong or right answers,

just what you think', people can still unconsciously be seeking clues as to whether they are giving the 'right' responses.

EXAMPLE: William can be characterized as having a strong personality, but even he was affected by this. Note in this example how a short question from the interviewer seeking clarification about the identity of a brother inadvertently changes the course of the narrative. William is talking about the death of his father:

> *William:* . . . and left my mother with the two dogs, and one, one of my brothers . . .
> *Interviewer:* That's the brother that had the mental breakdown?
> *William:* Yeah, it is, it is, yes. Eh [*cough*] [*cough*] My brother had a mental breakdown. He was the next brother to me. He did teaching at . . .

William dropped the account of his father's death and moved on to a description of the circumstances that led to his brother's mental breakdown. The point here is not that the course of an important narrative was lost (it may have been, but it was replaced by another narrative that William also found salient) but rather that a relatively minor intervention from the interviewer produced a significant and unintentional shift in the course of the interview.

Some interviewees thrive when put in the situation of having an attentive audience to whom they can hold forth on their favourite subject – themselves. This will not be the case for everyone however. For others, a completely non-directive approach will not work at all and some sort of questioning or eliciting information will be necessary.

The problem becomes one of how to ask questions that are non-directive – questions that do not direct the respondent towards topic areas predetermined by the researcher as being of importance – with the end result being that the researcher's preconceptions, at least to the significant topics, are confirmed. How does one maintain the inductive generation of concepts that is at the core of the realist approach?

Since one must ask *something*, a possible strategy is to ask about neutral facts that can be presumed with some justification to be of significance to almost everyone. For example, the chronological details of a person's educational or job history, whether they are married and have children and so on can be asked about. The hope is that the factual reply will lead on to a more discursive response. The problem remains, however, that this is to some extent imposing preconceptions.

A second solution is to have in reserve some neutral questions that might lead to introspective or unanticipated answers and hence to a more genuinely non-directed response. For instance, a 40-year-old woman can be asked: 'What was the most important thing that happened to you in your 20s?' We do not know what her reply might be. Hopefully, something of significance did happen during that decade and her relation of it will act as a springboard to further topics.[19]

As discussed in more depth in the analysis chapter, when one is employing the realist/grounded theory approach, the analyst uses the non-directive information collected in an initial interview to generate basic generalizations or proto-concepts. These abstractions from concrete data are then checked immediately by testing them empirically – either by reanalysis of the interview transcript or a second interview. So, the realist researcher will return to his/her respondent for a second interview. The format of this second interview will differ in that this time the interviewer will be asking specific questions based upon ideas or proto-concepts that the first interview suggested.

This raises practical considerations for the timing of interview and re-interview. The format of the second interview will be governed by what is revealed during the initial analysis of the first interview. Hence, the researcher must allow sufficient time for the first interview to be transcribed and analysed. To rush the process, and carry out the re-interview prematurely invalidates the logic of the grounded theory analysis procedure. Without adequate preparation, the second interview may produce a greater bulk of material but is unlikely to be efficient at yielding extra insights.

EXAMPLE: In his first interview, William spoke about people who 'follow that education curve'. The examples he gave, both in general and with specific reference to his own brothers and sisters, were about people who leave Northern Ireland in order to do their higher education in Britain and then settle down there, never to return. For example:

My mother was very concerned where my youngest sister Margaret would go . . . Margaret at one stage was keen to go to Sheffield. . . . [The] fear was that she would, eh, that if she had gone to somewhere across the water[20] she wouldn't come back. And this is something that is very common amongst Protestant kids who go to grammar school, go to university in England and Scotland and just don't come back, settle down, have a life, make friends etc. settle down and then get a job, get established. Eh, and certainly, I'm quite sure it's probably the same would have happened to me if I'd gone to Edinburgh, eh, but I came up, did my Accountancy in Belfast, got my first job in Belfast with the Executive, second job in Belfast, third job in Belfast and now I live in Belfast. . . .

One interpretation of the above and similar excerpts is that William was talking about 'the Ulster diaspora', the general tendency for middle-class (Protestant) youth to leave Northern Ireland to do their further education in Britain and then to be lost to the province when they settle there permanently (Miller et al., 1993). An alternative interpretation of the same excerpts could be, however, that William was putting forward a more general idea of 'inertia' in life trajectories – a tendency for people to settle into a career pattern early on which is then hard to break. Protestant youth moving temporarily to Britain for education and then finding themselves settled there decades later could be specific instances of a general phenomenon in William's eyes. This led on to questioning in a later interview to establish whether the specific or general conception held for William and about how he saw the dynamics driving the progression of careers.[21]

As the number of cases being interviewed by the realist researcher grows, the concepts and ideas being generated from new cases should begin to approach 'saturation' – rather than completely new ideas appearing, one should be seeing confirmation of ideas that have been noted before, or 'variations on a (already existing) theme'. These 'saturated ideas' could form the basis of questions for first interviews with later respondents in instances where the non-directive phase of the first interview is completed fairly quickly (in effect, telescoping the second interview into the first) or where a respondent dries up later on in an interview and needs 'pump-priming'.

Interviewing – neo-positivist approach

Neo-positivists employ a deductive mode of interviewing that is soundly based in pre-existing concepts and theory. This is in marked contrast to the inductive, grounded theory mode employed by adherents to the realist approach. The preliminary groundwork for an interview in the neo-positivist style will adhere most closely to the classical hypothesis-testing paradigm in social science. Neo-positivist biographical research will be soundly anchored in an existing body of social concepts and theory. The researcher will have primed himself/herself with a review of relevant research literature. The strategy of interviewing or the questions used may be a conscious replication of a previous study. Before carrying out any interviews, the researcher will have developed a semi-structured 'interview schedule'. This will be organized as a series of topics for which information will be sought. The topics will have been developed from pre-existing conceptual literature and, where the literature is extensive, can often be quite detailed. The interviewer may have prepared specific questions about important items. There is a clear rationale of *'accumulation'* driving the design of the interview schedule – the information that the research is designed to elicit will either be a confirmation or testing of findings established elsewhere or a direct addition to existing knowledge. Gaps or 'logical next steps' in existing theorization will be providing the guidelines for the design of the current study. The study of gender and political participation in Northern Ireland that the author was involved in fell solidly within the neo-positivist paradigm. A review of existing literature had established at the outset of the project that the then current research literature on political participation was largely confined to conventional 'malestream' conceptions of political activity. A large body of theoretical literature that criticized this male bias did exist but this conceptual critique had not been backed up by empirical work employing more 'gender neutral' measures of public participation. The author's study was designed explictly to fill this gap. The quantitative survey filled part of the gap by providing estimates of the parameters of public participation of women and men when more inclusive measures of activity were developed and deployed. The quantitative survey, however, could not adequately

cover topics such as the motivation underlying political participation or how some individuals became active while others
from very similar backgrounds did not. This latter gap led to in-
depth interviews with 'the active' that included the taking of a
political life history. Being based in the conceptual critique of
'malestream' political science, the semi-structured interview
schedule that provided the basis for the in-depth interviews
was designed along decidedly neo-positivist lines. For instance,
one of the main factors that the literature put forward as a
hypothetical explanation for women's lower level of participation in public life was their domestic responsibilities. This led
in the design of the interview schedule to the inclusion of
prominent sections devoted to domestic issues such as questions about the effect of child-rearing upon public participation,
the division of domestic responsibility in relation to activities
outside the home, and so on.[22]

The use of a semi-structured interview schedule does not
mean that one simply is employing a somewhat long-winded
version of a survey questionnaire however. A semi-structured
life history interview in the neo-positivist mode will be prefaced
by a carefully designed introductory statement. This statement
will explain the subject of the interview to the respondent and
set up the context in which questions will be asked. By explaining the overall rationale of the interview, the subsequent questions should have 'face validity', or seem legitimate. What the
introductory statement must not do is inform the respondent
about what the interviewer expects the pattern of responses to
be.

Neither does the interviewer slavishly follow the ordering of
questions on a semi-structured interview schedule, dutifully
recording each answer in time-honoured survey tradition.
Rather the questions contained in a semi-structured schedule
should be seen as 'jumping off points' designed to spark
responses from the interviewee. Although questions specifically
about a given topic exist prior to the commencement of an
interview, the mode of interviewing remains non-directive.
Lengthy, discursive answers are the goal. If the respondent goes
off on a tangent, this is permitted (in fact, encouraged) as long
as their digression has some sort of relevance to the topics of the
interview. The questions of a semi-structured interview schedule are best seen as a checklist of topics that need to be covered

by the end of the interview. Not all questions need to be asked, nor does the order of questioning on the interview schedule need to be followed slavishly. If the interviewee thoroughly covers all of the topics implied in the interview schedule with little or no prompting from the set questions, so much the better. The schedule acts as a backup or 'insurance policy' to ensure that all of the points deemed significant on conceptual grounds at the outset of the study are covered in interviews. It is much more desirable if the respondent spontaneously moves to topics without the necessity of an explicit prompt from the interview schedule.

The situation can arise where a respondent does not cover a hoped-for topic spontaneously and then provides only a cursory answer to a prompt. At this point, the interviewer may need to resort to probing in order to secure more complete information. Here, the interviewer is faced with the dilemma of eliciting more information but without leading the interviewee into producing responses that are predetermined by the questioning. One can use a technique of probing with increasing intensity, starting with an expectant glance or a 'pregnant pause', and gradually moving up to an explicit question (Fielding 1993: 140–41). The degree to which the interviewer will resort to explicit questioning will depend upon the importance of the area in which information is missing. Missing information from a crucial part of the study will necessitate more vigorous probing.

EXAMPLE: 'Social mobility' provided the general theoretical background for the neo-positivist interview of William. An important sub-topic within the area of intra-generational or career mobility was the extent to which particularism versus universalism had dominated William's job movements throughout his career. This included establishing whether William had secured his jobs through personal contacts or networks or through more universal means, such as applying for publicly advertised jobs in which appointment would be made on the basis of interview. Here, the interviewer is probing to establish whether William's job moves were determined by 'universalistic' or 'particularistic' criteria.

> *Interviewer*: So you were in the Executive. You started there when you were on placement [*immediately post-university degree, in order to obtain professional qualification*]?

William: I did about eighteen months in the Executive, approximately just over a year with the Board, and approximately eight and a half years with the Council. All basically what you'd call local government.

Interviewer: And the contacts from each job sort of lead into the other one because they all were similar work?

William: Well, similar work to a certain extent. . . . [*discussion of pension scheme*].

Interviewer: Was it because of the experience you have? When you try to get into other jobs you have the kind of experience.

William: I have.

Interviewer: The experience they're looking for?

William: That's right. That's right. I've worked along. I have very good experience in the Executive. I obviously knew the ropes and the interview panel, they thought I could do the job. I went to the Board, eh, I was only there for a relatively short period of time. I think I did relatively well and, obviously, when I went along for the interview for the Council, the ironic bit about it, I heard later on that I actually beat somebody for the job who was much older than me and much more experienced, but they appeared to like the fact that I'd been fairly active and had done a fair amount of work in my previous jobs. . . .

Interviewer: Yes, so . . . did you see it advertised?

William: Yes, advertised in the paper.

Interviewer: So it wasn't a matter of word of mouth?

William: No, it was quite clearly in . . . I mean, when I worked in the Executive, I couldn't even have told where the Board accountants were based. I didn't even know that. I knew where the headquarters were, and I met some of the accountants. I didn't even know where the accountants were based. Similarly, when I worked for the Board, even though I was probably only a quarter of a mile away from there, the [*Council*] accountants' office, I didn't even know where it was.

Interviewer: You didn't know people who worked in the office there?

William: I didn't know anybody. You know, I mean, there was no sort of even, eh, . . . nobody at all . . . you know.

Interviewer: It was on your own bat.

William: It was on my own bat, absolutely nobody whatsoever. Actually, it wasn't as if there were strings pulled or anything like that there, eh . . . in terms there were no strings, in terms of those

two jobs, it was just purely by interview that I got the jobs . . .
[*William then moves to an account of what it was like to be the new
person in a large office.*]

Interviewing – Narrative approach

The initial stage of a narrative-style interview can resemble that
for either a realist or neo-positivist interview. In their first
interview, the narrativist may adopt the non-directive, grounded
theory strategy that would employed by a realist and carry
out an unfocused, non-directive interview. If the narrativist is
seeking to test or confirm a body of concepts or theory, he/she
may resort to questioning, but the goal of these direct probes is
to elicit further narratives (Rosenthal and Bar-On 1992: 109).
Where the narrativist approach begins to differ from that of
realists or neo-positivists during the conduct of the interview is
in the primacy which the narrativist approach accords to the
interaction between interviewer and interviewee. While neo-
positivists and even realists may in the end have to fall back on
a series of invasive questions, these questions and the focus of
the interview are always directed *at* the respondent. If you read
the transcript of a realist or neo-positivist interview, you might
learn a great deal about the person being interviewed, but you
should discover little about the researcher as an individual. In
their pure forms, the realist and neo-positivist approaches both
see any effects that the interviewer as a person may be having
upon the responses given by the interviewee as 'contamination'
of the data. In this respect, the realist and neo-positivist views
of interviewing are the same as those of quantitative survey
researchers. For narrativists, the true focus of the interview is
upon what realists and neo-positivists regard as contamination
– the interviewer/interviewee interaction. 'Treating interviewing as a social encounter in which knowledge is constructed
suggests the possibility that the interview is not merely a
neutral conduit or source of distortion, but is instead a site
of, and occasion for, producing reportable knowledge itself'
(Holstein and Gubrium 1997: 113–14). This does not mean that
the information that the respondent gives is seen as insig-
nificant or false – the goals of maintaining accuracy and com-
pleteness still hold. What is different, however, is that what
constitutes a truthful and accurate account is dependent upon

the situation at the time of the interview. What is 'true' when the respondent talks to Interviewer X on Day 1 at Location A may not be what is 'true' when the same respondent talks to Interviewer Y on Day 2 at Location B. No one is lying (we hope!),[23] it is just that the story the respondent will tell will shift with the passing of time and changes in location,[24] and a main effect upon how the interviewee responds at any given time will be the interplay between him/her and the interviewer. The effects this has upon analysis will be discussed later, here we will consider how these considerations affect the manner in which one carries out interviews.

The implications for interviewing of adopting the narrative approach range along a continuum from a minimal to a high level of involvement and interaction between the interviewer and interviewee. One can adopt the narrative approach and at the same time maintain that the interviewer should keep their personal distance just as with the realist and neo-positivist approaches. The interplay between interviewer and interviewee will be a central concern, but not until analysis. This minimal adoption of the narrative approach advocates non-involvement as an ideal but considers this ideal to be unattainable. That is, the interviewer's characteristics are bound to affect the course the interview will take and this must be recognized.

Most proponents of the narrative approach, however, do argue for at least some relaxation of the prohibition of interviewer effects. The most prominent advocacy of a maximum interplay between interviewer and interviewee is associated with feminist research methodology. Genuine human interaction between the interviewer and interviewee is taken as axiomatic. Stanley and Wise (1993), writing from a feminist perspective, make a strong statement of the position that would be held in common by narrativists generally:

> [In mainstream research] 'Emotional involvement', the presence of emotions, is taboo; and an ideology exists which states that it is *possible*, not just preferable, to prevent this from happening. But we say that this is mere mythology. . . . 'The researched' will have feelings about us as much as we will about them, and also feelings (and theories) about the research itself. . . . Our experiences suggest that 'hygienic research' is a reconstructed logic, a mythology which presents an oversimplistic account of research. It is also extremely

misleading, in that it emphasizes the 'objective' presence of the researcher and suggests that she [sic] can be 'there' without having any greater involvement than simple presence. In contrast we emphasize that all research involves as its basis, an interaction, a relationship, between researcher and researched. . . . this necessarily involves the presence of the researcher *as a person*. Personhood cannot be left behind, cannot be left out of the research process. And so we insist that it must be capitalized upon, it must be made full use of. . . .

We see the presence of the researcher's self as central in all research. One's self can't be left behind, it can only be omitted from discussions and written accounts of the research process. But it *is* an omission, a failure to discuss something which has been present within the research itself. The researcher may be unwilling to admit this, or unable to see its importance, but it nevertheless remains so. (Stanley and Wise 1993: 160–61, emphasis in original)

Feminist research methodologists have put forward strong critiques of the power relationships that exist in a 'normal' interview situation (for example, Oakley 1981). They point out that social scientists have advantages over their research subjects. Due to their knowledge of the research literature, they are almost bound to know more about the topic of their research than their respondents. Their intimate knowledge of their own research project and its goals will give them a further advantage that can only be partially redressed by an attempt to explain the goals of the research in layperson's terms. This is compounded if the goals and purposes of the research are kept secret from the research subjects, which is often the case. Furthermore, the researcher by definition is likely to be more formally educated than his/her subjects and, being a middle-class academic, is often also much better off, of a higher social status, and socially secure.

All this leads to unequal power being implicit in the research relationship and, with inequality, the potential for exploitation of the research subject. Implicit within the narrative approach is the argument that the researcher must take steps to redress the inequities in the research relationship. 'Informed consent' is even more a sought-after goal than normal. At the onset of the interview the researcher needs to explain the goals and purposes of the research as comprehensively as possible. Deliberate omission of details or misleading the subject about the purposes of the research are to be avoided.

In addition, the researcher needs to emphasize the points where they and the research subjects are on common ground; for instance, in feminist research, emphasizing that both the researcher and her subjects are women and subject to the constraints of a patriarchal society, albeit at different levels (Cook and Fonow 1990). The usual constraints against researchers revealing personal details about themselves are relaxed and the sharing of the researcher's personal history may even be encouraged (Reinharz 1992: 67–72).

'Normally' if a situation arises in which the active intervention or assistance of the researcher could result in a material change for the better for the respondent, this should not be done except in cases of dire necessity because the intervention would be an artificial alteration of the situation. ('Normal' ethics does mandate that the researcher intervene, but only *after* data collection is concluded.) Advocates of the complete interventionist stream would argue that withholding help, even temporarily, is an exploitation of the unequal power relationship between researcher and researched. If they have the means to do so, the researcher has an ethical duty to provide assistance to the researched. This duty overrides the potential damage to the research project that might arise from a so-called 'contamination' of the data.[25] So, adopting the narrative approach does imply (though not mandate) a relaxation of the typical constraints against allowing the interviewer to reveal personal details about themselves. The narrative approach is centred upon a focus on the interplay between interviewer and interviewee that will be discussed later in Chapter 5.

Transcripts of the first interviews can be used to facilitate the narrative approach. A respondent can be shown the transcript of the initial interview. This allows the interviewee to comment upon the accuracy of the first interview and in addition can lead to a reflexive account of the same material. In effect, a second, repeat, interview is being carried out. This can be taken further if the researcher elects to show the respondent preliminary interpretations of the first interviews – a significant extension of the research process. By inviting the respondent to comment on interpretations and analysis as well as just transcripts, the researcher is bringing the interviewee into the research analysis.

This incorporation of the respondent can be extended throughout the analysis and can go as far as including respondents in the production of material for publication and/or giving them the right to comment on or veto the final drafts of published material.

A concluding ethical note

The extension of the respondent's involvement to the stage of analysis raises a number of ethical issues. On the one hand, the respondent is empowered. He/she is given the opportunity to exercise a (perhaps considerable) degree of control over the use to which their interview material will be put. 'Informed consent' becomes more realistic when the respondent has the possibility of following, and affecting, the production of material from the investigation through to its fruition. On the other hand, the respondent cannot be an uninterested participant and is put in a more exposed position than the academic researcher. There are psychological pitfalls that are a potential danger with any life history interview and these pitfalls loom deeper if the researcher chooses to involve respondents in depth in the interpretative process. Firstly, the giving of a life history is an introspective process for the interviewee, a forced introspective process that people do not normally go through. It is naïve to believe that introspection is always a positive experience – it *may* be positive, but the alternative is also possible. Life history interviewing is invasive, old hurts or traumas may be reopened or unfavourable comparisons with more successful compatriots or with alternative life paths that may have been more fruitful are a real possibility. The truth does not necessarily set one free. One may take stock and realize that the sum total of life's accounts are wanting. An older person may have the realization forced home that most of their life is now past. Secondly, some respondents may agree to participate in a life history study in the belief that the experience will be therapeutic. After all, the interview is being conducted by a social scientist and the collection of the life history in interview does somewhat have the appearance of psychotherapy. However, no therapy is being given; the collection of a life history is just that, a one-way process.[26] False hopes may be raised.

The possible vulnerability of participants in a biographical study means that the usual strictures about giving potential participants in a study a clear enough explanation so that they can exercise truly informed consent deserve even more emphasis than usual. As well as taking care during the collection of information, researchers should ensure that the closing of the interview relationship is done with care and should make it possible for respondents to contact the research team at a later date.

Once the first interviews are collected and transcribed, the researcher will be moving to the central phase of the research – the analysis of the data.

Appendix 1 – Interviewing Exercises

No amount of discussion or text material on interviewing can substitute for the experience of actually carrying out an interview. In order to give you a realistic experience of life history interviewing, two interviews will be carried out in this exercise. The first will be an unfocused interview either about your interviewee's general life history or a topic chosen by you. After you carry out a preliminary analysis, you will carry out a second interview with the same respondent which will be based upon material collected during the first interview.

Choosing an interviewee

If you are going through the chapters in sequence and already have carried out the 'family history chart' exercise in Chapter 3, the person you choose for life history interviews should be someone on the chart. If you did not collect a family history, you will need to find a 'victim'! Your instructor may have suggestions about locating potential respondents or may have set up an arrangement for interviews (for example, with the occupants of a retirement home). Basically, anyone may be an appropriate subject for these interviews – except for the constraint that they must be old enough to have had a life to be interviewed about. That is, interviewing a fellow student will not be an option unless that student is older than the typical university-age person.

Choosing a topic

If your respondent is someone drawn from your family history chart, a suitable topic could be one of the suggested areas of interest for family history research given in Chapter 3. You may have noticed something unusual or interesting about 'your' family when you were collecting the material for their grid that may form a suitable focus for a life history interview. An alternative is to carry out general life history interviews with 'your' family member in which the family grid only acts as background.

If your respondent is not drawn from a family history grid, you can opt for a general life history or choose to carry out the interviews on a topic of your own choice. Your instructor may have a list of suggested topics or a single topic that will provide the basis of interviews carried out by the whole class. One possibility may be to combine this interviewing exercise with other parts of your course. You may be expected to carry out an individual research project as part of your degree requirements. The life history interviews may be suitable as the fieldwork for such a research project. Other courses you are taking may provide inspiration for a topic for the interviews here. The literature and conceptual issues covered on another course can form the background and context for the life history interviews.

Interview 1

The purpose of the first interview is to give you the experience of carrying out an unfocused life history interview. You will need to make preparations beforehand. Your respondent will need a carefully worded, non-directive explanation at the beginning to get them started. While the interview is to be unfocused, most respondents will need prompts to keep them going. Your goal is to obtain a comprehensive account of their life or of the topic area of their life that you have selected from their perspective. Hence, non-directive prompts will have to be prepared carefully so that the final result has been affected as little by you as possible.

If possible, you should tape the whole interview. If that cannot be done, you must take thorough notes, either during the interview or immediately afterward.

Between interviews

A preliminary analysis should be carried out between interviews in order to lay the groundwork for the second interview. If you were able to tape the first interview, you should prepare a transcript of at least ten minutes of talking time from an important part of the tape. (Ideally, you should transcribe the whole tape. To require this, however, would impose a heavy burden.) The purpose of this transcription is to give you practical experience of transcribing (which can be a revelation) and to provide some written material from your own interview for analysis.

Using the grounded theory-type techniques of the realist method (discussed in Chapter 5), carry out a preliminary analysis of your transcript or notes. If you have not transcribed the whole tape, you still can use the untranscribed material by listening to the tape and making notes. The purpose of this preliminary analysis is to lay the groundwork for a second interview.

Interview 2

Based upon the results of your preliminary analysis, prepare a semi-structured interview schedule. If your interviews are centred upon a specific topic, you also can use your knowledge of the social science thinking on that topic to help you set questions. These questions will provide a framework for the second interview. *Do not carry out the second interview until the semi-structured interview schedule, and you, are ready.*

The style of interviewing in the second interview will be quite different. The semi-structured interview schedule will provide the basis for direct questioning and probing as you attempt to fill any gaps in your knowledge that you identified after the first interview. In this second interview, you can be much more 'interventionist' – reacting directly to what your interviewee says, probing actively for more information, telling them what you think etc. As before, tape the interview or at least take extensive notes. The material you have collected in these interviews will be used in the analysis exercises at the end of the next chapter.

For this exercise, turn in your transcript and/or interview notes and the semi-structured interview schedule. This should be accompanied by a reflective account of what took place during the two interviews that includes the following questions:

- How did you choose your interviewee and make the initial approach?
- Did the interviews go well or not so well? Were you able to put the interviewee at ease? Were they (too) talkative or reserved? Did you have to 'move the interviews along' with probes or prompts, and were these effective?
- 'What sort of things particularly influenced the flow and content of the interview, for example, location, noise, faltering or intrusive (tape recording) equipment, you or your interviewee's lack of confidence, rapport, body language' and so on (Wilton 1998: 29).
- Did some questions seem to work better than others? Why do you think this was so?
- What were your feelings about being an interviewer?
- Did any (unexpected) problems or issues arise?

Please give a realistic account of how well the interviews went. Since this is designed to be a learning exercise and it is difficult to anticipate beforehand how a respondent will react to being interviewed, do not feel that you have to report a 'perfect' interview. What is important is that you have learned from the experience.

Appendix 2 – On Transcription Conventions

There is no single set of agreed conventions that one can follow when transcribing an interview. Nevertheless, there are elements and features of 'good practice' that are common to most the transcriptions that are published (Riessman 1990). The following should be taken as guidelines only and can be adapted to suit one's own needs and preferences:

1   Each speaker should be identified clearly. When a new speaker starts, go to a new line.
2   Transcription should be literal, *how* a person says something as much as what they say can provide valuable insights. Poor grammar, pauses, and so on should be left in and not 'corrected'.
3   Non-verbal sounds, such as coughs and laughs should be recorded, but inside square brackets to prevent their confusion with the text.
4   Pauses should be shown: short spaces of silence by dots, with each dot indicating one second; longer silences inside square brackets with the length of the silence indicated. Verbal pauses (for example, *eh, um*) can be shown in the text like words.
5   Words especially emphasized by the speaker can be underlined or put in FULL CAPITALS (*italics* should not be used since some computer programs for analyzing qualitative data do not recognize *italics*).
6   If material cannot be heard on the tape, this should be indicated in square brackets.

EXAMPLE:

> *Interviewer*: When you went to primary school, did your parents help you a lot or were there particular teachers in the school?
> *William*: Well [cough] basically worked seven grades at primary school. Eh, . . . we had some very good teachers at that school, and in particular the one who took us . . . for P7. Eh, an English guy called Smith . . . Mr Smith. His daughter was actually [could not understand] in our class. And P6 we were taken by a . . . teacher that was Mrs Douglas, and <u>coincidentally</u> her daughter Ellen was [laugh] in the same class as me. So two of the girls in my class were both taught by their parents.

Transcription symbols can be extremely precise and detailed. For examples drawn from conversation analysis, see Psathas (1995: 70–78) and Heritage (1997: 254).

Notes

[1] The ideal method for monitoring an individual's experience of effects of change across time would be a proper longitudinal study

where the person is followed across a lengthy span of time – years or decades. Practical difficulties, however, mean that longitudinal studies will always be rare. In a true longitudinal study there will be a very long time lag between the beginning of research and the reporting of results. Financial costs, maintaining a committed research team across years, managing to find a funding body willing to make the very long-term or open-ended commitment necessary to fund the research, the difficulty of identifying suitable individuals for study at the outset (for example, how does one identify likely international migrants years before they decide to move?), and keeping the same respondents committed to the study involved over a span of years all conspire to keep true longitudinal studies rare. One perhaps may come across a serendipitous source of longitudinal biography (for example, the long-term diary of a migrant), but a long-term qualitative longitudinal study consciously designed from the outset is another matter.

[2] The reader will note that these sentences open up a number of issues that are of great significance for a biographical researcher – the extent of accuracy in an individual's perception of social structure, whether respondents can give reliable accounts of their past perceptions or the strategies they employed or rejected at some previous time. These issues are important, but they are fundamentally analytical issues and as such are better left to the next chapter. For reasons of presentation, this text will maintain a division between issues of data collection in this chapter and issues of analysis in the next. In practice, the two overlap.

[3] Again, issues are being raised here that have important implications for analysis. The three basic approaches to the biographical perspective deal with the malleable way in which respondents can construct their life histories/stories in quite different fashions.

[4] The author has supervised students' undergraduate research dissertations over a number of years. A number of good project topics regularly come about from students realizing that personal contacts form the potential for a project. For example, one student carried out a life history study of child sexual abuse in which the respondent was a close friend. (This particular project also raised ethical issues not encountered by the 'typical' undergraduate in that it became evident during the fieldwork that contact between the research subject and professional counselling needed to be established.)

[5] Selective or judgemental sampling is akin to the grounded theory technique of theoretical sampling. Theoretical sampling, however, is a more general technique. In theoretical sampling, the units can be individual people, but the units sampled also could be particular contexts or locales, certain types of behaviour, pertinent sections of an interview transcript and so on. The point of theoretical sampling in grounded theory is that items are chosen on conceptual grounds to provide additional information or data that is needed to broaden or refine a developing theoretical schema.

[6] 'Saturation' is one of the main procedures used in the realist/grounded theory approach to establish the validity of analysis results. It will be discussed at greater length in Chapter 5.

[7] With the partial exception of stratified probability sampling where the population is divided into some conceptually based groups, or strata, before elements are randomly chosen from each strata.

[8] But note that locating a potential candidate for an interview and securing their agreement are not the same thing.

[9] This issue will be returned to under 'Ethics' below.

[10] Note that the strategy of leaving the most 'difficult' questions to the end when the interviewee may be more willing or motivated to answer is a form of manipulation of the subject, even if the manipulation is justified by the need to secure complete information.

[11] The possibility that a social researcher could claim 'professional confidence' as grounds for withholding field notes or interview transcripts from a criminal investigation is debatable – possibly in the United States, certainly not in the United Kingdom or Ireland.

[12] Segments can be missing from transcripts due to their being illegible on the tape. The interviewee may be able to remember what they said at a crucial missing segment. William was given a copy of his interview transcripts and was appalled at his poor grammar. He wanted to edit the complete transcript in order to 'improve' his grammar but eventually accepted assurances he was not unusual and that normal speech does not conform to good grammatical practice.

[13] The copyright of direct quotes remains with the person who said them; so a respondent has a legal right to require the removal of any direct quotes. Agreeing to give an interview does imply that the respondent did not object to direct quotation. If the researcher neither misled the respondent nor gave an undertaking not to use direct quotes, the interviewee probably cannot claim their rights were violated if they delay their objections until after a publication has appeared.

[14] Note also that the computer programs developed for the analysis of qualitative data may require that transcripts conform to a standard format of conventions.

[15] Parts of this subsection were greatly assisted by the excellent discussion of oral history interviewing in Paul Thompson's *The Voice of the Past* (1988).

[16] This paragraph is written with reference to the most unstructured, interactive formats of life story interviewing. Life history interviews also can be highly structured with a definite 'list' of points or topics that must be covered (though with the *proviso* that digressions are allowed) and with the interviewer maintaining as low a profile as possible, keeping their own personal interventions in the interview to an absolute minimum. The points that follow would carry even more force in an approach to interviewing that subscribes to these latter constraints.

[17] There is no such thing as a completely unfocused interview, however. In order to start, the interviewer will have had to identify themselves as a researcher, to have given some sort of explanation about the purpose of the research, to have asked a starting question. All this, along with the practical actions, such as a formal request for an interview and setting up a tape recorder, will establish the context of an interview (Thompson 1988: 199).

[18] The interviewer was lucky in that, even after that fairly incoherent introduction, William commenced a long and detailed account of his life that required little prompting. He began with his birth, but immediately went back to *before* his birth and gave an account of how his father and mother met.

[19] For extensive batteries of potential life history questions, including some designed to produce discursive responses see Atkinson (1998: 42–53) and Thompson (1988: 296–306).

[20] People in Northern Ireland routinely refer to Britain as 'across the water'.

[21] This further interviewing established that the more circumscribed conception of 'education curve' – a phenomenon that specifically applied to the migration of Protestant youth to Britain – was the one held by William.

[22] The results revealed a complex pattern. For instance, publicly active women who had had children did curtail their activities, but only when the children were young. Being a mother was often cited as a motivation for public activity. A simple 'either/or' model of public activity within couples did not hold. If one's spouse was active, this promoted one's own activity and domestic duties were shared. For an extensive report of the study, see Miller et al. (1996).

[23] Though deliberate falsification on the part of the interviewee – lying – can be easily accommodated within the standpoint of the narrative approach; see Chapter 5.

[24] 'Changing location' can mean changes in *social* position as well as geographic movement.

[25] The question of active intervention has been with qualitative research since its beginnings. During the fieldwork for the classic study of *Street Corner Society*, the researcher William Foote Whyte was asked to act as secretary for a community and social club because of his educational background (Whyte 1955). He was reluctant to take this on since his active involvement would lead to an alteration of the situation.

[26] The alternative, that the interviewer attempts to offer some half-baked advice or unqualified 'pop therapy' is much worse.

5

Analysing Life Histories

CONTENTS

What animal walks on four legs at dawn, two legs at noon and on three in the evening? – 'The Riddle of the Sphinx'

Students are often given the task of carrying out an independent research project 'on a topic of their own choice using a research method of their own choosing'. The same students probably will have had some research methods training that included an introduction to the statistical analysis of quantitative data. Most students placed in this situation will recoil from the idea of voluntarily lumbering themselves with a repetition of a difficult and stressful experience and instead of picking a statistical project will opt for the 'easier' choice of qualitative research. At the beginning, things seem to proceed quite smoothly. Their chosen topic is one that is intrinsically interesting to them. There are obvious commonsensical connections between the conceptual ideas they are investigating and the behaviours they observe or the questions and answers produced by interviews. Students who have chosen a qualitative method in the cynical anticipation that a qualitative project would involve less work seem to have their expectations rewarded. At that point, however, things begin to go wrong.

Students who have taped interviews and then elect to transcribe them, discover that transcription is a long, slow and tedious process. The sheer mass of qualitative information is daunting, even if it is only notes from a limited amount of observation or a small number of interviews. It is unclear how one goes about combining into a coherent structure the rich detail that even a small amount of qualitative fieldwork will amass. Questions of proof or disproof, relatively clear in a statistical test, are not so straightforward with qualitative data. The relationship between concepts and the information held in the data becomes hazy. Supervisors may begin to make disturbing suggestions that computer programs for the analysis of qualitative data should be employed. For the student who expected an easy ride, the realization slowly dawns that, while qualitative research might require less effort at the stage of collecting data, there really is no such thing as a free lunch and 'pay back' time can come at the stage of analysis. An in-depth qualitative analysis can be a much more involved and developmental affair than a quantitative statistical study.[1] The collection of life stories or family histories by their nature implies the collection of large and complicated amounts of rich data; so the problems of a complex qualitative analysis are likely to be compounded if one undertakes biographical research.

Analysis

Following the structure of previous chapters, the three approaches to the biographical perspective – realist, neo-positivist, and narrative – will be given in turn. As in previous chapters, the reader should note that this formal division into three approaches is a heuristic device for the purposes of instruction. Researchers are not required to maintain the tripartite division employed here and may mix and match techniques pragmatically. One should note also that the division between the previous chapter on interviewing and data collection and this chapter on analysis is an artificial construct. Real researchers are unlikely to wait until all their data collection and interviewing is complete before commencing analysis. In fact, the opposite practice – early analysis of the data from first interviews in order to provide feedback for subsequent data collection – is the preferred option.

The realist approach

Realists follow the canons of the grounded theory approach to the analysis of qualitative data. The process is one of induction – a gradual process of abstraction in which one moves from literal empirical observations toward abstract concepts. The key point is that of constantly evaluating the developing concepts in the light of concrete data – hence 'grounding' the theory in data.

If the realist approach is applied in its pure form, the initial interview will be as non-directive and as unfocused as possible. The first stage of analysis will be a broad scan of the interviewee's account, which hopefully will be as close to a monologue as possible. This initial scan primarily will be a sorting exercise in which the respondent's account is grouped into sets of pragmatic categories. These categories arise from the nature of the account with their structure being either one used by the respondent to order their account or a preliminary system of *ad hoc* organization that develops as the researcher goes through the transcript. It is very unlikely that the preliminary categories arrived at in this manner fall into a single coherent system. More likely is that a jumble of several separate proto-systems appear. The structure of these systems will be 'flat' – that is, they probably will be little more than a set of 'pigeonholes' in which to insert portions of the transcript with very little, if any, structure of sub-categories. The ideas or principles underlying different systems may be mutually contradictory. Certain passages or blocks of monologue may overlap or be used in different systems in completely different manners. A coherent 'chunk' of monologue under one system may be broken down into parts that go into different headings under a competing system. It is likely that a large amount of material remains free-standing – perhaps of significance but apparently not 'fitting' with anything else.

EXAMPLE: William's first interview was unfocused and unstructured in that William was asked to give a general account of his life. He proved more than equal to the task and talked for more than two-and-a-half hours with only a minimal amount of prompting from the interviewer. The resulting transcript ranged widely over his life and background. William structured his account chronologically, he began with his parents meeting and gradually worked his way up to the present, moving through his own childhood, education, university days and early career to the present. Throughout the account, he often mentioned members of his family as they had been at that time in his own life. This led to two initial sets of proto-categorizations: one based upon the type of family member being discussed – grandparent, parent, aunt or uncle, sibling, wife and son – and the other upon the stages of William's life trajectory. Other major sets of categorizations grew out of the latter part of the interview – most notably sports and activities in the public realm (to be discussed below).

The results of this first 'pass' through the data form the building blocks for the beginning of an analysis. The next stage is to re-sort the material in the transcript into the preliminary category systems. (Material falling into more than one set of categories will be duplicated and placed in each.) The respondent is likely to have jumped from topic to topic, sometimes returning to something discussed earlier. This sorting exercise, bringing together all of the passages that seem to relate to a particular category, hopefully should make it easier for the researcher to notice patterns implicit in the data. At this stage, the possibilities opened up by the re-sorting mean that the first real *concept work* may take place.

The analyst can refine a categorization system further. Once all the material relevant to a heading is brought together, it should be possible to notice potential ways of organizing the material under a single heading into a more detailed set of sub-categories. (As before, it may be that more than one way of organizing the data appears.)

Reorganization under a broad heading may point to gaps in material. The existing set of *ad hoc* headings represented in the data may imply the existence of others that are absent or missing altogether. For instance, when the material about William's family members was brought together and sub-categorized by relation, it became apparent that under 'Parents' the amount of coverage given by William to his father was much greater than that relating to his mother. This suggested a subsequent line of questioning.

The areas of overlap at which material falls into two or more separate systems may give clues about how to refine a conceptual system further. The overlap may indicate that the two separate proto-systems can be seen as sub-sets of an overarching 'meta-category'. The material that has been 'left over' – portions of the transcript that seemed to stand alone or not fall into any overarching system of categorization – can be looked at again as a single body of material. At this point, some unattributed material may begin to 'fit' within an existing system. Since the gross volume of this unattributed material is less than the complete transcript, it also may be possible to see patterns that previously had been obscure. That which previously seemed irrelevant or trivial may no longer appear to be so. This can lead to the reattribution of some of the unassigned material into new category groupings.

EXAMPLE: From the first pass through the data, it became evident that sports, and one sport in particular – running/ athletics – figured very prominently in William's account. The whole interview was peppered with references and lengthy expositions about the place of athletics in William's life. Hence, a broad category, 'Sport', was created and all references to sport were collected together with an initial set of sub-categories of each specific sport mentioned: running/athletics; rugby; golf; and skiing. Once the sports references were brought together, it became immediately apparent that sports, especially running, intersected with practically all facets of William's life. William's father had run as a young man and encouraged his son:

> He [*William's father*] attended Trinity College, Dublin and had been involved in athletics and showed an interest in running, and even as a small boy he would take me over to . . . one of the . . . big clubs in Ireland, in those days it was Bann Running Club. And I was certainly always attracted to that, so, in due course when the opportunity arose, I got involved in running.

Sports made up a prominent part of the culture of the grammar school at which William boarded. When William went to university, his social life centred around athletics and rugby. Many of the social contacts that William formed at university have been maintained over the years through his continued involvement in running, first as a competitor and later as a club officer and organizer of events.

> I continued to run for Queen's . . . [*cough*] I was in the Irish squad, but I really never got any further than that in terms of Irish representation. And at that stage, eh . . . the only really open club was called Belfast Running. This club was situated in an area that . . . the paramilitaries . . . in no uncertain terms told the local runners to move out. That club went into great decline . . . though we were working very hard. We (*re*)established ourselves. . . . I joined that club before I left Queen's and I was heavily involved on the committee as it made that transition from eh . . . a club that had no premises to quite fine premises on _____ new equipment, and the club was reborn. And I was also involved as an accountant, eh . . . in doing the books. . . . Treasurer for one year . . . ah . . . and have always been heavily involved in running the bar, in the running aspects of the club administration, and a number of years ago I was, eh, Vice-President for three years, and then I was President for three years . . . and I was heavily involved in the . . . writing of the constitution. [*cough*] And over the years I've had a number of involvements with sport in running. [*William's account at this point continued with mention of his involvement with all-Ireland sporting bodies and his setting up and managing a number of running events in Belfast over the years.*] William met his wife at a function of the athletics club.

The social contacts that existed through his sporting activities proved important for William when he moved into private practice as an accountant.

> I have to say that a lot of people I run with, that I know . . . I've done a lot of work for, for instance, . . . I've done work for people in the running club, and then their neighbours would come to me and say, '*OK, you've done a good job for them, can you do a good job for me?*' So, it's basically by word of mouth, but the initial, eh, exposure has been through running. A lot of my contemporaries have come to me and asked me for advice and a lot has come of that. So there has been a, a certain overlap there which has been beneficial to me. . . . Well, I'm not, I mean, I'm not, I didn't join the running club to, . . . make contacts. I mean, it was always, I

have always enjoyed the running, and the contacts have been a nice spin-off I have to say.

William's high level of involvement in organizing athletics in Northern Ireland evolved into involvement in other types of public activities that are not related directly to sports.

Some of them really developed, eh, . . . socially developed through the running. My position on the Lagan Valley Regional Park [*a committee set up by the government to consider the development of a regional parkland area*] I was proposed by _____, who is on the Sports Council who met me through my involvement with the running committee.

At this point, the rudimentary sport classification was recast. Both in terms of the sheer amount of his narrative that William devoted to athletics and in the way he kept returning to the topic, sport appeared as an organizing principle in William's life of equal (and perhaps more) significance as his career, or his family. The breakdown by type of sport was relegated to a secondary level and involvement in athletics was made a major category. The sub-categories were altered to reflect the ways in which sport intersected with other aspects of William's life history: family background; schooling; university; social life; career and work; other public activities.

The grounded theory approach is to move continuously from data to theory and back again. Theory is 'grounded' in data in that it arises directly from observations and then is immediately validated by cross-checking the newly derived abstractions against existing empirical material. In the analysis of interviews, this is done either by looking for material in the existing transcripts that will have a bearing on the concepts being developed or, if additional interviewing is an option, framing questions or probes that are designed to generate additional material relevant to the concept.

Both of these procedures were followed with William. For instance, two of the new sub-categories created by the recasting under the broad heading of 'Sport' were 'Business/Career' and 'Social networks'. Furthermore, sometimes these two sub-categories overlapped to produce a group that could be labelled 'Business connections'. For example:

> I've derived a lot of work from running, the running community.
> Therefore that wave of running goes through my life in terms of
> work. Eh, there is also that sort of thing, there is that social thing,
> . . . you can also find it in terms, in terms of rugby clubs as well.
> And all sports tend to be, keep work within their own com-
> munities. . . . Some of these guys I run with. . . . If we didn't get
> on with them socially, they wouldn't be recommending me.

The transcript was interrogated in more depth to establish the
extent of overlap between business and social contacts formed
through sports. Firstly, the material already categorized under
the 'Sport' heading and under either 'Business/Career' or
'Social networks' but not overlapping with 'Sport' was looked
at closely to see if any additional overlaps had been missed.
Secondly, portions of the transcript that were coded as
'Business/Career' or 'Social networks' but not under the broad
'Sport' heading were looked at to see if there were 'business
connection' overlaps outside the context of sport. A number of
these were found, but, interestingly, all except one of these were
concerned with William's career prior to his leaving the public
sector and setting up in private practice. The end result of these
latter exercises was that for the period after he entered private
practice only one passage was found in which 'Business/
Career' overlapped with 'Social networks' that did not also fall
under the 'Sport' heading. Although it may not have been a
deliberate strategy on his part, contacts formed through his
sporting activities have been important for William's success in
private practice.

Prompted by preliminary findings, questions that explicitly
probed for the role of social connections in business were
included in William's second interview. This questioning in the
latter interviews confirmed the connections between social and
business contacts taking place within the sport context as being
a special feature of William's private employment. These latter
questions broadly confirmed the earlier findings. Here, William
is speaking about his organization of running events:

> When I organize events, I try to do them so they run well. . . .
> Therefore hoping that then reflects on my professional expertise.
> . . . I have a lot of expertise . . . so I'm trying to use that expertise
> to make events . . . go better, and, I also like to think [*that people*

will say] 'He organizes these well, I hope then when it comes to doing the books for our business, he'll do those well.' Eh, it's a logical consequence.

But William did express some ambivalence. When asked directly whether there were drawbacks to mixing business and social contacts, William told about a conflict that arose when he recommended a sub-contractor to a client:

We were all involved in running, and it also became quite difficult to become critical of him [*the sub-contractor*] in as much from two points of view. I knew him socially through running and I'd been a friend of his for many a year, and the other aspect was, in terms of my . . . feeling that I wanted to deliver a good job for my client.

The above cycle – validating provisional conceptual constructs against empirical material (in the case of life history research, interview notes), refining or proposing new constructs on the basis of that validation – can be repeated indefinitely. The endpoint of a stage of analysis begins to come into view as the researcher approaches 'saturation'. At some point the collection of new empirical material does not add significantly to the process of concept generation. The new material slots into the existing conceptual frameworks, validating them but not throwing up anomalous instances. Since new empirical material ceases to challenge the existing conceptual frameworks, its collection does not spur further development but rather can be seen as 'variations on (pre)existing themes'. At this point the data can be said to be 'saturated' and the further collection of information[2] is no longer necessary. The most obvious instance of saturation would be a study in which interviews have been carried out with a large number of individuals making up the target group of the research. At some point, the information gleaned from interviews with new individuals can be slotted into existing frameworks. The new cases are 'new', but only in the sense that they are *additional* – they are not generating new material that requires conceptual development for its incorporation. The Bertaux-Wiame study of French bakers provides a clear-cut instance of saturation in this sense.

While we were conducting our fieldwork, however, we came to realize that a process was taking shape. . . . This new process could be summarized by saying that every new life story was confirming what the preceding ones had shown. Again and again we were collecting the same story about poor, usually rural backgrounds, about very hard exploitation and training during apprenticeship; about moving from village to town, from town to city, from city to Paris. . . . Again and again we heard about some specific health problems. . . . And despite our efforts, we still could not find a single adult bakery worker born in Paris or even in its suburbs. What was taking place was a process of *saturation*: on it rests the validity of our sociological assumptions. . . . at the beginning of a research project, one is too ignorant to interpret all the signs and understand their sociological meaning. In order to establish what is particular to a given life and what is a consequence of socio-structural relations, i.e. what is relevant to sociological thinking, one has to move from one life story to another, trying to diversify as much as possible the cases observed, until the *process of saturation* takes shape. When certain elements show up with regularity, when saturation makes it obvious that facts such as long hours, rural origins, health problems and geographical migration are not due to chance personal characteristics or individual decisions but instead to certain structural features, one may begin to develop sociological assumptions about the sociostructural features which might lie behind these recurrent observed facts. (Bertaux and Bertaux-Wiame 1981b: 187–88; see also Bertaux and Bertaux-Wiame 1981a: 179)

Repeated interviews with a single individual or a small set of individuals can reach saturation in a similar manner. When additional interviews with the same person only generate repetitions of the same information, data saturation is being reached.

EXAMPLE: William gave an account of his job history in his first interview. In this account William mentioned two points at which his career could have taken different paths. When he was seeking his first job in the labour market, William was interviewed and turned down for a post in a private accountancy firm. Subsequently, he was offered, and accepted, employment as an accountant working in a large public body. Only a few days after taking up the latter post, the private firm contacted William and offered him a job, which he declined. Some ten years later a similar career division point occurred. William had concluded that promotion prospects within the public body that he then worked for would not open up for some years and this was a significant factor in a decision to enter private practice. Shortly after he had left and moved into private practice, a number of senior accountancy positions in the public body that he had left unexpectedly became vacant.

In the analysis of the interview, these portions of Willam's account were coded together under a heading of 'Ambition' and a provisional sub-heading of 'Choices'. Since it was not clear from the original accounts whether William saw these points of divergence as missed opportunities or merely as points at which his career could have taken an alternative course, the following question was asked in a later interview: *Do you have any regrets about your career?* William answered in the affirmative and spontaneously related two, and only two, incidents from his career – the same two that had prompted the question. Hence, the conjecture that William did see these particular points in his work history as missed opportunities was confirmed. Saturation can be demonstrated in the close parallels between William's first and second accounts of these points in his career. Taking William's accounts of this career start:

First interview

I had an interview with the Executive, eh, and about the same time I had an interview with a guy in, eh, [*mixed up talking*] in a firm of private accountants as opposed to local government. And, eh, I had a good interview with this chap. . . . he said, 'Basically, I'm looking for more experience' than I had. . . . Ultimately the funny bit about it, just after I started with the Executive, within three or four days, he wrote to me, and said a second job had become available. Now, the funny thing about it, I worked for local government for ten years [*before going into private practice*]. If I'd joined him I'd probably had an entirely different career direction. I would have gone in private practice, say worked there for five years, become a partner. If he might have retired, I might have taken over the practice. It's quite a busy commercial practice, but, just by the fact the Executive offered me the job first, I accepted that. . . . but that's just one of those things, the quirks of life, you know.

Second interview

I was interviewed for a job just before I got my Executive job, my very first job, and I just missed out on that, and I often thought, well, that would have been into private practice at a very early age, and I would have had a totally different career life. And I don't really think very often how that would have gone, because that's just pointless, to go back through your life.

Then, William's accounts of the time when he decided to leave the public sector and move into private practice:

First interview

The Assistant Chief Accountant retired. I applied for that job, and one of the others, there was three of us who . . . obviously were graded Senior Accountants, I was the youngest. I applied for the job of Assistant Chief Accountant, didn't get it. I'd have been surprised if I'd got it. And one of the other two guys got it. So, to a certain extent, eh, . . . you know, eh, my next step had been blocked, and to a certain extent I didn't see any immediate way of that being cleared. Although ironically, shortly after I left, one of the other accountants got the job. The Assistant's, the Assistant, sorry, the Assistant Chief Accountant, he moved. . . . His post became available. He [*the third original applicant*] applied for the post and got it. So, if I had just stayed a bit longer, I might have gone further up the organization. If fact, I'm pretty certain I would have done. . . . I just, I took that conscious decision to leave and, well, sort of you make your bed and lie in it. So that's just one of those things.

Second interview

I often muse that, if I'd stayed in the Council, where I would be now. Eh, that's one that I wouldn't say regrets, but, eh,. . . . I, I would sort of, I say, muse about it or, you know, sort of, '*Where would I be now?*' Let's see, if I'd be there, I'd be, let's see now. So and so moved on. I could have been Assistant Chief Accountant. He retired, as did the Chief Architect. Then there's a Director, Director of Services. Could I have got his job? You know, and I often muse, eh, fantasize even, dream, you know. Not, not very often, but I often think, 'Where could I have been now?' Some of the guys [*tell me*] 'If you'd be here now, you'd be doing such and such a job, you know.' I have a reasonable organizational skill which is recognized there, but I decided to, eh, try life outside. . . .

> Not as successful as it should have been, but my, that's, some-
> times a lot of it comes down to luck, the breaks you get, and
> sometimes, perhaps, the, the dice hasn't rolled as well for me, but
> I, I mean, I'm not, I don't regret it at all. But I do, I do sort of
> muse.

Note that saturation as discussed above refers to the collection
of data and not to the analysis process itself. When the collection
of additional information begins to fail to produce genuinely
'new' material but only repetitions of similar empirical material,
saturation is being reached. 'For most theory-building researchers, data collection continues "until theoretical saturation takes
place." This simply means (within the limits of available time
and money that the researcher finds that no new data are being
unearthed. Any new data would only add, in a minor way, to
the many variations of major patterns' (Strauss and Corbin
1998: 292). The cycle of concept generation and validation also
may reach saturation and cease to produce significant incre-
ments in concept development.

Saturation can be an indicator of the point at which fieldwork
can cease, but recognizing an endpoint to an analysis is not
so easy however. Coming to a stopping point or dead end in
theory generation may be only a temporary hiatus. Sharing
the material with a colleague, a comment made at a seminar
presentation or in a referee's review, or just 'sleeping on it' over
a weekend or a few days may produce an insight that can lead
to a breakthrough and a whole new spate of concept development. An analysis may never be complete in the sense of final-
ized. Rather than completion, perhaps a more realistic goal is to
strive to identify when the analysis has reached a stage suitable
for presentation to a wider audience.

Neo-positivist

The deductive, theory-testing stance adopted by the neo-
positivist approach to the analysis of qualitative data stands in
marked contrast to the inductive, grounded theory procedures
used by realists. The starting point for neo-positivists is theory.
The questions that make up the semi-structured schedule used
as the basis of a neo-positivist interview have their inspiration
in a pre-existing body of concepts. While the neo-positivist

analyst allows for serendipity and the generation of new theory, the core of the analytic process is the validation and extension of existing conceptual constructs. The nature of a transcript will differ from that produced by an unfocused realist-style interview. While the answers given by the respondent may be discursive and rambling – he/she literally is a *respondent* – the text has been sparked in response to a series of questions designed to probe issues determined by theoretical concerns. The initial coding pass through the transcript of a first interview will be different from that done by a realist analyst. The coder will be working to a predetermined conceptually based structure of categories. The initial coding pass essentially will be a sorting procedure – checking to see whether each of the predetermined topic areas has in fact been covered at some point or points in the interview. The omission or inadequate coverage of an area may need to be rectified in a subsequent interview.

The neo-positivist interview with William was centred around the topic of social mobility with particular emphasis upon the role of primary contacts (family, friends and personal acquaintances) in mobility. Additional questions were framed in order to tap important areas of existing theorization about social mobility – for example, the role of cultural and social capital in promoting upward mobility, the effects of changes in social structure upon mobility.

The initial 'sorting' exercise into theoretically predetermined categories pointed up some gaps in the data. For example, questioning about the parents made up a prominent section of the interview. Upon completion of the preliminary coding pass, it was apparent that a much greater bulk of more detailed material had been collected about the father in comparison to the mother. This could either be a genuine result – that William's father in fact was more influential upon him than his mother – or an artefact of the interview – that the nature of the questioning inadvertently had led William to discuss his father more or that William's emphasis upon his father was due to a bias on William's part in favour of talking about his father. These considerations led to additional questioning in a later interview that probed specifically for the mother's influence upon William.

This probing did produce more material on the mother – especially with regard to her helping her children during their primary education – but also produced even more material on the father. William tended to answer a direct question about his mother and then expand his answer by shifting to his father.

> EXAMPLE: *Interviewer*: What about your mother? What sort of influence did she have on you, say, in your education or your early childhood?
>
> *William*: She very much pushed for us all to have a good education. I would say my parents made a lot of sacrifices financially, in terms of what others in their peer group were achieving in the area . . . They had, my father, eh, always drove a fairly modest car . . . but then, being a GP. . . .
>
> [*later in the interview, after an additional probe about the mother's influence on his education*] She would write these all out and she would go through these and she was very much, you know, impress us, spelling and things like that. So, there was a very strong influence from that point of view. Certainly as far as the eleven-plus exam. Eh, my father was always extremely busy . . . in terms of his medical . . . commitments and really did not spend that much time looking after our education. He very much delegated that to my mother . . .

While probing for the mother's role did elicit more material, the net effect was to confirm the initial hypothesis that his father had more influence upon William.

Once sorting is complete, the next stage of analysis in the neo-positivist approach is one of validation. Does the material collected on a given topic coincide with what one would anticipate from existing theory? In effect, a hypothesis-testing mode is being employed where, if the empirical data match that which has been anticipated, the theory rests on firmer ground than before.

The actions taken if the empirical observations do *not* fit with the theoretical predictions, however, demonstrate how the neo-positivist approach is not just a sterile transplant of quantitative techniques to textual data. Rather than stopping short if the hypothetical predictions are not met by the observations, the lack of a fit between observed and predicted responses prompts the analyst to move to a grounded theory mode – generating or reformulating concepts.

> EXAMPLE: William's response to a question designed to elicit material on structural mobility provides an interesting case in

point. Structural mobility, a concept developed by the quantitative study of occupational mobility, refers to changes in the odds of being mobile from one type of occupational strata to another that are caused by alterations in the occupational structure of a society. A clear example is the enormous increase in the relative proportion of white-collar and upper middle-class jobs during the twentieth century. Much upward mobility can be attributed to people moving up into the middle classes in order to fill ever-larger numbers of newly existing white-collar positions. William's family seems basically to confirm this pattern (his grandparents' generation was mainly farmers or police, William's own generation is almost all professionals), but note his response to a direct question about the effects of structural change upon his own career.

> [Today] There is an awful, awful lot more accountants than there was, eh, when I came into the profession. . . . [laugh] There's too many. Less accountants would be more. . . . even though the work's grown, eh, there are more, eh, I think, I think there is, eh, an excess of accountants. That's my personal viewpoint. And how is that? That is also expressed in terms of remuneration. In other words, eh, if there's five accountants for five jobs, well, you're all going to get a piece, a cut of the cake. If there's six accountants for five jobs, well I don't want to lose out. I'm going to cut my fees to make sure I get a job. If there's ten accountants for five jobs, you know, it's become a lot more competitive.

On the one hand, William is confirming the existence of structural effects; by his reckoning, the number of accountants has risen.[3] At the same time, however, he is raising deeper issues about the implications of a disproportionate increase in the number of accountants. Too many accountants is leading to increased competition and a significant drop in the individual fee income of most accountants. If William's perceptions are correct, a refinement of the theory around the concept of structural mobility is suggested – the unlimited expansion of upper middle class strata may have the effect of causing the living standards of these strata to fall, hence bringing into question whether movement into a falling stratum should be considered upward social mobility. (A number of authors in recent years have begun to question the assumption of never-ending upward structural mobility, for example, Goldthorpe 1985; Miller 1998.)

So, while the initial stage of a neo-positivist analysis will differ markedly from that followed by realists, the approach followed by neo-positivists can move towards grounded theory-type procedures after the initial sorting into categories. If the interviews have gone well and generate material that, rather than just confirming what was expected beforehand, challenges the expectations formed at the outset, the convergence with a grounded theory mode of analysis will be more pronounced and ultimately more fruitful.

Narrative approach

> The narrative dimension [of] the life story aims, by means of a coherent and global process, to account for the whole of the informant's life experience until the moment of the interview. This means that the narrative encompasses not only the temporal and causal organization of facts and events considered significant, but also the value judgements that make sense of this particular life experience. In turn, such a view implies that the most crucial information resides not in the answers given to specific questions, but rather in the narrative organization itself. (Chanfrault-Duchet, 1991: 77)

In the narrative approach to life history analysis, the view of the nature of data (the text of interviews given when a life story is taken) differs fundamentally from that taken by the realist and neo-positivist approaches. While the former two approaches vary in the starting points from which they begin to deal with data – the realist approach using an inductive, grounded theory-building logic and the neo-positivist approach employing a deductive, theory-testing logic – each shares a common standpoint on the nature of the reality they are trying to comprehend. There is a definitive reality that, while it may never be comprehended in its totality, constitutes a goal that one attempts to draw near to when carrying out the theory-building procedures of a realist or the theory-testing procedures of a neo-positivist analysis. Subjectivity, either of the interviewee or of the researcher, is, ultimately, a problem that the analyst must attempt to curb.

> The narrative approach turns this view of subjectivity on its head. Rather than being a problem, subjectivity, the manner in which the respondent perceives his/her situation and activities in social structures and networks, is the very stuff of analysis.
>
> The neo-positivist research tradition would regard this aspect as an irritant that must be eliminated, reduced, or at least controlled. In our view, trying to eliminate a 'problem' such as this amounts to a quixotic fight against imagined giants, giants that in the final analysis are revealed to be not even windmills but rather the 'winds' of the everyday world. The 'wind' driving the mill that is creating biographical constructs cannot be eliminated without eliminating the constructs themselves, because this wind is in fact the ongoing interaction between the biographer and his or her social world. Life stories, taken as constructs, are inseparable from these interactional processes; they themselves evolve out of the genetic process of interaction, just as their presentation in the biographical research interview is a product of the interaction between narrator and listener. (Rosenthal, 1993: 64–65)

Situation and structure affect an individual's subjective viewpoint, but they do not determine it in a unilateral, unvarying way. Within constraints, subjective perception is malleable. This has the effect of shifting the focus of an analysis towards the manner in which the respondent has negotiated his/her unique view. The negotiation is ongoing and never finally resolved, so a person's subjective view will not remain static. As well, 'when reconstructing the narrated life story we have to take into account another phenomenon: Each interview is a product of the mutual interaction between speaker and listener' (Rosenthal 1993: 64). The researcher in the act of conducting an interview will be affecting the respondent's negotiation – producing a Hawthorne effect[4] or a social version of Heisenberg's Uncertainty Principle.[5] In fact, since interviewing is directed straight at obtaining the views of the respondent, it has more of an effect on the subject's perceptions than the normal bumps and grinds of everyday life. The inherently invasive nature of interviewing means that the narrative approach must place special emphasis on the interaction between interviewee and interviewer.

These features of the narrative approach – taking the standpoint that 'reality' is malleable and multiple and a focus upon social aspects of the interaction between the interviewee and interviewer – do not mean that the narrative approach sees social reality as being completely fluid. A respondent's situation in social structures and networks will impose parameters upon their freedom of manoeuvre, even though the options may remain wide. For instance, three individuals may discover that they are terminally ill from an incurable form of cancer. One reacts by availing themselves of all the pain-deadening drugs they can procure and withdraws from all social activities. A second refuses to accept the diagnosis and spends their last days trying one quack cure after another. A third resolves to live as fully as possible during the time left to them. While the reactions to being terminally ill differ profoundly, in the end, each will die.[6] The narrative approach emphasizes the subjective negotiation between the individual and their situation, but it is not counterfactual.

A narrative analysis can be thought of as having a triangular structure. One apex of the triangle is the respondent with their pre-existing subjective and negotiated view of social reality. A second apex of the triangle is the interviewer with an agenda of research interests and goals. The responses to the interviewer's questioning produce the third apex of the triangle. The manner

Respondent,
with pre-existing subjective and negotiated view of reality

Interviewer,
with research agenda and goals

Responses
to questions

FIGURE 5.1 *Triangular structure*

in which the respondent frames his/her responses to questions will be determined in great part by how they see the researcher and the effect they calculate their responses will have. A 'double hermeneutic' is in operation here. The respondent's answers come out of their subjective perception of their situation in social networks and structure, *and* are cast with regard to their perception of the researcher's position relative to them and how they calculate their answers will be taken by the researcher. A similar 'double hermeneutic' is working upon the researcher. The interviewer will frame questions with regard to his/her perception of what the respondent is capable of providing information about, and also with regard to their perception of how the respondent sees the interviewer. For example, William was a middle-aged, university-educated married man employed in a professional occupation. One could anticipate that he would see his status as roughly equivalent to that of the researcher and this equivalence would affect the manner in which the interview proceeded – both in the stance adopted by the interviewer and the manner in which William replied. Similarly, William's undirected life story could be anticipated to tell about, among other things, his education, career and family. It would have been remarkable if it did not and this would have prompted further investigation.

These considerations form the conceptual underpinning for a distinctive style of analysis of narrative interviews. The respondent has their own subjective awareness of their placement or social situation and sees their status in relation to their perception of the interviewer's placement. In the same manner, the researcher evaluates the answers of the respondent at two levels, reportage of social situation, but reportage that has been mediated by the respondent's evaluation of his/her position relative to the researcher. This technique overlaps with the 'objective hermeneutic' method (Rosenthal 1993: 89; Chanfrault-Duchet 1995: 218). 'Objective' since the analysis proceeds on a step-by-step basis, with each supposition or proto-hypothesis being immediately evaluated against interview transcript material. 'Hermeneutic' since the researcher is aware that any material being produced by the interviewee has been generated with regard to both the interviewee's subjective perception of his/her situation and history and the interviewee's perception of the researcher and the relationship between the two of them.

Finally, the researcher himself/herself will filter the material selectively through the mesh of their own perceptions at the stage of analysis; hence, 'objective hermeneutics'.

This approach begins with a technique of 'narrative interviewing' that corresponds to the non-directed interview technique described in the previous chapter.

> The aim of this interview method is to elicit and maintain a full narration by the interviewee, with the help of non-interfering techniques applied by the trained interviewer. The method is based on the assumption that the narration of an experience comes closest to the experience itself. Narration of biographical events gives the chance to glimpse some of the motives and interpretations guiding the actions of the biographer [the interviewee].' (Rosenthal 1993: 89–90; Rosenthal 1991: 34)

> The main theoretical principle is . . . the idea that there is a 'gestalt' (a whole which is more than the sum of its parts; an order or hidden agenda) informing each person's life that it is the job of biographers to elicit intact and not destroy through following their own concerns (Rosenthal 1990; see also Rosenthal 1991: 34). . . . Broadly, their [narrative interviewers'] strategy can be summarized in terms of four simple principles: use open-ended not closed questions, elicit stories, avoid 'why' questions, and follow up using respondents' ordering/phrasing. . . . The art and the skill of the exercise is to assist narrators to say more about their lives (to assist the emergence of their gestalt) without imposing the interviewer's own relevancies (thus destroying the interviewee's gestalt). (Holloway and Jefferson 1997: 60; see also Bertaux and Kohli 1984: 224)

The analysis proceeds at three levels. Firstly, the biographical life history is constructed. That is, the factual details of the respondent's life are clarified and ordered into the correct temporal sequence (Rosenthal and Bar-On 1992: 10). In the case of William, this stage would be mapping out the factual details of his life in chronological order – the places he has lived in, the schools he attended, the educational attainments and examinations he passed, the sequence of jobs he held in the public sector before moving into private practice, his history of sporting activity, both as a competitor and then as an organiser of events, information about his other extensive public activities, his marriage and the birth of his son and so on. The bulk of this information normally comes from the interviews, but note that much of it in theory could be obtained from other sources of data such as school records or the minutes of club meetings. Procuring additional factual information about the respondent from sources other than the interviews is not ruled out. Note also that this type of factual information is that which has been collected by quantitative survey studies of life histories.

Secondly, the collation of factual information lays the ground for the second stage of analysis – *thematic field analysis*. An interviewee, asked to tell the story of their whole life, cannot relate everything – to do so would literally take longer than the living of it.[7] The interviewee must choose what areas to concentrate upon and how to frame the presentation of these areas to the interviewer. 'The narrated life story thus represents a sequence of mutually interrelated themes which, between them, form a dense network of interconnected cross-references' (Rosenthal and Bar-On 1992: 111). Lives contain what is for all practical purposes an infinite number of events and occurrences. Any person faced with relating the story of their life must edit what they tell (Breckner 1998: 5). They will be selective in the events they choose as relevant and then in the manner they choose to relate them. Memory itself is notoriously selective. Much salient material simply may be not recalled due to the course of questioning that the interview takes or simply just forgotten. Memory recall is malleable; the past is being constantly rewritten by the subject as some events fade and others grow in significance. The 'facts' recalled may be wrong, warped by social prohibitions or reinterpreted due to intervening events. The interviewer can affect how the material is related. Incorporating these considerations and the factors of interviewee/ interviewer interaction noted above makes the method truly qualitative.

> The purpose of the analysis of the narrated life story is the reconstruction of the present meanings of experiences. . . . The analysis is particularly concerned with discovering the mechanisms of selection guiding the biographer's [interviewee's] choice of textual elements (or stories) in relation to the general thematic orientation. . . .
>
> The present perspective determines what the subject considers biographically relevant, how he or she develops thematic and

temporal links between various experiences, and how past, present, or anticipated future realities influence the personal interpretation of the meaning of life. We can thus assume that the process of selection being carried out by the biographer while presenting his or her life story is not haphazard or arbitrary, merely reflecting possible interactive influences of the interview situation or a passing mood. A life story does not consist of an atomistic chain of experiences, whose meaning is created at the moment of their articulation, but is rather a process taking place simultaneously against the backdrop of a biographical structure of meaning, which determines the selection of the individual episodes presented, and within the context of the interaction with a listener. (Rosenthal 1993: 61–63)

The factual framework of the life history acts as a template against which the areas that the interviewee chooses to emphasize or skip over can be evaluated. Sections of the text resulting from a non-focused interview can be categorized by the modes of narration used by the interviewee into three types:

1 *Description*, where the interviewee's intention is clarification or to report factual information. 'The decisive feature distinguishing them from narrative is that descriptions present static structures' (Kallmeyer and Schütze 1977: 201, cited in Rosenthal 1993: 89);
2 *Narration*, where the interviewee adopts a story-telling mode – 'sequences of actual or fictitious occurrences that are related to one another through a series of temporal or causal links' (Rosenthal 1993: 89) – in order to place an event or sequence of events into a structure which is intended to convey a thematic point to the listener;
3 *Argumentation*, where the interviewee's intention is to assert one particular viewpoint or interpretation when several alternative views are possible or where he/she anticipates scepticism or rejection by the listener.

Note that the essential determining factor for each mode of address is the intended or anticipated effect that the interviewee wants to have upon the interviewer/listener. 'The reference to past events occurs in the context of the present situation, and under the criterion of their significance to it' (Kohli 1981: 67).

Interviewees are not giving their accounts in a vacuum, everything they say is being said with regard to how it will be taken by the listener/researcher.

Thirdly, proponents of this approach argue that results of the thematic analysis make it possible for the researcher to dig deeper and draw conclusions about the state of mind and reasoning of the respondent in the past at the time that events took place. 'After the thematic field analysis . . . the task is to reconstruct the perspective of the past, to reconstruct the biographical meaning that the experiences had at the time they happened' (Rosenthal 1993: 68–9).[8]

A development from the general objective hermeneutic mode of analysis has been the use of 'micro-analysis' to place selected sections of text under intense scrutiny. In the course of the analysis of an interview, certain points in the interview may come to stand out as being particularly significant for providing insight into the topic of the research. A block of these crucial passages may be selected for special treatment.

The micro-analysis duplicates the general objective hermeneutic procedure, but within the chosen passages. The units of analysis are extremely small – sentences, lines or phrases. The first unit (say, a single sentence) is looked at in isolation, without any preview of the units to come and without any back reference to the text that may have preceded it. All possible interpretations of the meaning of this first unit are made. These possible interpretations in effect constitute a series of proto-hypotheses about the meaning of the unit and about the likely content of the units to come. Then the next unit is looked at and the process of attaching all possible interpretations is repeated, only with the proviso that interpretations derived from the first unit are now 'admissible evidence'. What should happen is that some of the previous interpretations are no longer tenable, proto-hypotheses that have been eliminated. Some previous interpretations still hold as possible explanations of what is going on, and hence are proto-hypotheses that now sit on firmer empirical ground. Thirdly, there will now be some new interpretations that have arisen from taking the first two analysis units into account together. The analysis then moves to the third text unit and the process is repeated.

Rosenthal (1993) has laid out a general routine and considerations to be followed at the stage of analysis of text units:

The narrative segments are categorized according to the various styles of narration, such as whether they are reported (sequences of events are chained together without expanding upon individual situations) or whether the biographer picks out individual situations to elaborate in detail and tells a story. The analysis of the sequentialization thus necessarily follows the structure of the text, each individual sequence being interpreted as it arises. The possible significance of each sequence to be interpreted is then considered without reference to or knowledge of subsequent units.

The following questions guide the hypotheses that are developed:

1   Is the biographer [interviewee] generating a narrative or being carried along by a narrative flow in the story telling?
2   How much is the biographer [interviewee] oriented to the relevance system of the interviewer and how much to his or her own?
3   In which thematic field is the single sequence embedded? What is the hidden agenda?
4   Why is the biographer [interviewee] using this specific sort of text to present the experience or theme?
5   Which topics are addressed? Which biographical experiences, events, and periods are covered, and what is left out? What comes up in the second part of the interview (after further questioning by the interviewer) that had been omitted in the first part, the 'main narration' (after the initial opening question)?
6   In which details are the single experiences or themes presented and why?

All possible hypotheses about each sequence are formulated: for each hypothesis a follow-up hypothesis is considered according to 'what comes next in the text, if this reading proves to be plausible.' These hypotheses are then contrasted with the text sequences that follow: Some of them gain plausibility whereas others are falsified. (Rosenthal 1993: 69–70; also Rosenthal and Bar-On 1992: 112)

'This line of reasoning' can be called 'the method of adduction.'

The micro-analysis continues until, ideally, only a single interpretation of the data continues to survive successive rounds of examination of new units and no new interpretations come from looking at new units. If this state is attained, the micro-analysis can be considered to have come to a successful conclusion.

What may happen, however, is that the micro-analysis will run out of relevant text units with a number of competing interpretations still surviving. In such cases, the analyst can try to locate other passages of text elsewhere in the transcript that would be relevant, and continue the micro-analysis with them. If no such passages exist, it may be necessary to reinterview the respondent using the endpoint of the analysis as the basis for lines of questioning. If neither extension to the analysis is an option and reviewing the existing data with the help of colleagues does not produce any solution to the impasse, one may be forced to accept that more than one plausible interpretation exists.

EXAMPLE: The following is an excerpt from the first, non-directed, interview with William that illustrates these principles of analysis. William is talking about his family [the notes in square brackets do not indicate breaks in text, but rather points in the analysis]:

[*Description/Report*]

My sister in Wales already had two, eh, had two children. They were my parents' first grandchildren, a . . . son, Gareth . . . and daughter, Kerrian, and, eh, so Charles [*William's son*] was born in January . . . '87.

[*Short narrative passage*]

Eh, I always recall it very well, one of these sort of happy things, of taking photographs, my father took photographs of Charles, he must have just been hours old.

[*STORY 1 – Set-up*]

Eh, my fa-, parents were having a fairly rough time, because one of my sons, one of my daughters [*laugh*] just correct it, one of my *brothers* was having mental breakdowns and quite a lot of angst.

[*Why the slip? Because William has to take on a paternal role?*]

And I know we went up to see him [*William's father*] on St. Patrick's Day . . . and, eh, I remember sitting thinking there I should take a picture of my father in colour. I never did. Eh, it was always something on my mind, because, eh, literally a few weeks later, eh, I was away skiing, and I came back off the plane, Mary [*William's wife*] was picking me up off the plane. She said,

[*Climax*]

'I have some bad news for you. Your father has just died of a massive heart attack.'

[*Resolution*]

So, he certainly went very quickly, very suddenly. He certainly didn't suffer, eh, eh,

[*Moral*]

and, as I say, that link between between the grandfather and the grandson was just lost, including the photographs we had just taken [*illegible*] . . . look back and thinking. And so, eh, my father died . . . and left my mother with the two dogs, and one, one of my brothers living up in next to me. [*End Story 1*]

Interviewer: That's not the brother that had the mental breakdown?

William: Yeah, it is, it is, yes. [*Report*]

[*STORY 2 (which commences directly after Story 1):*]

Eh, [*cough*] My brother had a mental breakdown. He was the next brother to me.

[*Report*]

He did teaching at, eh, what's known in history as the Polytechnic, it's the Jordanstown branch of the University of Ulster now.

[*Set-up*]

He took up teaching at _____ Secondary School, eh, a secondary school on the edge of Ballyhightown, not an extremely, no an area where kids just aren't motivated, and at that stage he was teaching kids, who were in what called, I always call it the remainder class, stands for remedial in school. They taught this crowd. They didn't get reinforced by government policy.

[*Argumentation 1 – Reasons why teaching atmosphere was bad*]

I suppose, fair enough, the kids were an extra year at at school, but these guys all knew they would go off as apprentices to joiners, whatever. I find it very rough going, and I think it probably got to him,

[*Argumentation 2 – Reason for brother's breakdown*]

so he, he packed in the teaching and took up chiropody. . . . So I say, my brother took up chiropody and at that stage, . . .

[*Climax*]

he had his mental breakdown, the first of many.

[*Resolution*]

Eh, it did affect the family in many ways. I had to go round to houses and answer calls and take him up to hospital, take him up to Gransha, the local mental hospital up outside Derry.

[Thematic analysis: The complete passage is about mortality and the change of generations. The death of William's father is juxtaposed against the birth of his son. At the beginning, William is one of the youngest generation. By the end of the passages, a new generation has arrived and he, as the eldest male in the family, has had to take on the responsibilities of his father, especially adopting a paternal role for his mentally ill brother.]

Life stories rather than life histories

A metaphor that helps to explain the distinction between the narrative approach and the realist and neo-positivist approaches is that of the life *story*. Following on from early biographical work, both the realist and neo-positivist approaches can be said to collect life *histories* – recollections of the empirical facts of a lifetime. Emphasis is placed upon the reliable and accurate recall of events. There is a supposition that a complete and total version of the life exists and the interviewing process is attempting to collect as much of that complete version as possible. In contrast, the narrative approach is different in that the respondent is seen to provide a life *story* – a *depiction* of the events of a lifetime. Unlike the life history which can be said to be a (hopefully accurate and reasonably complete) passive *re*construction of a core of factual events, the life story is an active *con*struction of the respondent's view of their life. There is no single 'best' or 'correct' construction. The content of a life story that a respondent will give in an interview will be dependent upon how they see their life at that particular moment and how they choose to depict that life view to the person carrying out the interview. The information given when a person tells their life story is 'true', but not in the sense of being a close approximation to a single omnipotent reality that would be 'truth' in the life history collected by a realist or neo-positivist. Rather, the life story is 'true' in that the story the respondent chooses to give at the moment of the interview is, at that place and time, the one they have selected as a genuine depiction of their life. In a benign sense, the respondent will slant their account to fit with what they see as being the interviewer's areas of interest and tell their story in a way that they believe will be sensible for the interviewer. The respondent also may choose to omit material that they do not wish the interviewer to know about or choose to lie deliberately. Faced with all of these considerations, the narrativist sees the interview situation as inevitably fluid. The only course in an analysis is to recognize the situational nature of a life story interview and to focus upon the dynamics that produced the unique situation of the interview that actually occurred.[9]

When relating their life stories, people literally will fit their lives into a story format – what Bourdieu called 'the biographical illusion'. Western creative fiction – from a short television advertisement for soap powder through to a highly intellectual novel – is dominated by conformity to a definite dramatic structure. A dramatic situation or tension is established, the tensions led to a period of confrontation or activity, eventually the period of activity concludes successfully or unsuccessfully, and this leads of a resolution of the conflict. A person relating their life story can attempt to impose this fictive structure upon their account.

Reissman lists a number of authors who have noted the literary conventions followed by the tellers of life stories:

> Like weight bearing walls, personal narratives depend on certain structures to hold them together. Stories told in conversation share common parameters, although they may be put together in contrasting ways and, as a result, point to different interpretations. Events become meaningful because of their placement in a narrative.
>
> Labov's (1972, 1982; Labov and Waletzky, 1967) structural approach is paradigmatic. . . . Narratives, he argues, have formal properties and each has a function. A 'fully formed' one includes six common elements: an abstract (summary of the substance of the narrative), orientation (time, place, situation, participants), complicating action (sequence of events), evaluation (significance and meaning of the action, attitude of the narrator), resolution (what finally happened), and coda (returns the perspective to the present). With these structures, a teller constructs a story from a primary

experience and interprets the significance of events in clauses and embedded evaluation. (Reissman, 1993: 18–19)

This is an especially strong statement of the use of literary structure, but the general point holds – that interviewees do use structural conventions when they tell narratives. For instance, William's life story begins with an account of how his father became a doctor and settled in the town where William was born. It continues with William attending a boarding school and developing an early interest in accountancy which he pursues through university. The period of conflict was William's early career as an accountant in several public organizations. The account of his career reaches a climax with a decision to move into private practice. An important sub-theme for William is his involvement in athletics which leads on into a high level of participation in public service. William then concludes by depicting his current life as a period of consolidation in which the public activities are being scaled down in order to give him more time to devote to his private practice and family life.

Real lives, however, are not acts of creative fiction and may not conform to this literary structure. They may be a linear progression through a life course made up of a number of stages without a centre or turning point. An uneventful or orderly life can go on for decades and then suddenly be transformed by a calamity that strikes randomly. Social reality may not conform to the socially structured depiction that a respondent feels compelled to put upon their life story; hence, the 'biographical illusion'.

While not disputing the factual nature of William's account, one can point out that the structure in which he has placed the account conforms to the literary stereotype of setting a scene, conflict/activity, resolution. If William had been interviewed 20 years ago, he probably would have given a different account in which the conflict phase would have been his progress through the educational system and obtaining professional qualification with getting his first job being the resolution. A quarter of a century from now, we would likely receive a different account in which the resolution could be entering retirement.

Narratives select the elements of the telling to confer meaning on prior events – events that may not have had such meaning at the time. This is a narrative transposition of Kierkegaard's famous statement that we live life forwards but understand it backwards. In understanding ourselves, we choose those facets of our experience that lead to the present and render our life story coherent. Only from a hermeneutic position are we poised to study the genesis and revision of people making sense of themselves.

Narrative models of knowing are models of process *in process.* . . . personal narratives describe the road to the present and point the way to the future. But the as-yet-unwritten future cannot be identical with the emerging plot and so the narrative is revised. (Josselson, 1995: 35)

One can take issue with Bourdieu's contention that the imposition by an individual of a literary structure of plot and theme onto their life is always a fiction. If a person believes a situation to be real, it can become real in its consequences. If a person believes his life to be following a specific pattern or reflecting certain themes, their actions in conformity to that belief can reinforce its reality. For instance, being a person who is competent in the public arena is a powerful part of William's self-perception of his identity.

'That's something that I' ve taken up myself. I' ve been . . . [*a lengthy account of committee activities in sports and the public arena follows*] That has all created, for lack of a better word, a committee animal. You know, you're prepared to go to a committee, you're prepared to work, you're prepared to achieve something'. [*This leads William to continue to put himself forward for public activities and to develop expertise that feeds back into more activities; for example,*] 'When I was asked to join the local housing association . . . I was prepared to get involved, to try and use my expertise to help'.

The narrative approach recognizes that the responses given by an interviewee can vary depending upon the interview situation. As discussed above, a source of this variability can be the interplay between the statuses of interviewee and interviewer and their perceptions of each other. The respondent's own subjective perception of their situation is neither necessarily constant nor even accurate. The stories that a respondent tells in interviews may shift or be mutually contradictory, even within the same interview. Unlike the realist and neo-positivist approaches, however, the malleability of the respondent's perceptions, and how they are shaped or contradict empirical facts, constitutes a main point of interest – in fact, the core of interpretation. As an example, let us take William's discussion of the status structure of his home town.

> EXAMPLE: *Interviewer*: Because he [*William's father*] was a doctor, do you think there was some sort of special social position that he occupied?
>
> *William*: Yes, without a doubt. In Larkissane the doctor was very, very, eh, special to his patients. Eh, it's a country practice. [*An account of William's father receiving gifts at Christmastime from patients and patients naming children delivered by William's father after him or after William and his siblings.*] And there definitely is a social position with regards to that in terms of the hierarchy of social life. . . . In terms of that social position. The school teacher was quite high up, as I can recall, in the late 50s and early 60s. The school teacher was on par with the sergeant, you know, the police sergeant. And they, I would consider, were higher than the bank managers. Now, that's all got turned on its head.

Note that the general discussion of relative statuses in the town was initiated largely by William himself. Secondly, William's account of the relative statuses of occupations by and large is inaccurate. School teachers rank somewhat higher than police sergeants, but bank managers always have been ranked considerably higher than the other two occupations (Jackson 1977). Thirdly, William's account of the relative statuses of the occupations is especially inaccurate for one occupation in particular, police sergeant. William went on to discuss a number of other occupations and policeman was the only non-white collar occupation mentioned. Why do policemen seem to hold a special position in William's *ad hoc* system of job statuses? One possibility is that this is just an idiosyncratic view that William holds and he happened to discuss police sergeants purely by chance. An alternative explanation, however, lies in the history of William's family. At least four members of the earlier generations of the family were police sergeants – both of William's grandfathers and two uncles. William's family in the past was a 'police family' and we seem to be seeing a hangover from that in the significance that William attaches to the profession. An apparent inaccuracy in the reportage of a status system in fact can be seen as an expression of a trend in the social mobility of William's family.

Conclusion

Analysts will follow different procedures depending upon which of the three approaches to the biographical perspective they adopt. In some respects the differences between the approaches will blur, particularly as an analysis proceeds beyond its first phases. The differences between the inductive, grounded theory-building techniques of the realist approach and the deductive, theory-testing techniques of neo-positivists will become less apparent in the latter stages of an analysis. Major proponents of the grounded theory approach have stated that their method does not start in a conceptual vacuum. For 'rhetorical purposes' and the desire to emphasize 'the need for grounded theories' at the time of its introduction, Glazer and Strauss, the originators of grounded theory, 'overplayed the inductive aspects' of grounded theory and 'greatly underplayed both the potential role of extant (grounded) theories and the unquestionable fact (and advantage) that trained researchers are theoretically sensitized. Researchers carry into their research the sensitizing possibilities of their training, reading, and research experience, as well as explicit theories that might be useful if played against sytematically gathered data.' (Strauss and Corbin, 1998: 166–67) Similarly, the realist analyst quickly will begin to generate concepts which must then be evaluated against empirical information in a deductive manner akin to neo-positivist hypothesis testing. Neo-positivists, in turn, quickly will begin to generate elaborations of concepts as refinements to theory arise from empirical material.

Any realist or neo-positivist analyst worth their salt will be acutely aware of the issues of subjectivity that form the core of the narrative approach. While the former may see subjectivity as problematic and the latter narrative approach sees subjectivity as the principle that informs an analysis, the difference on the ground may not be as pronounced as the formal tenets of the approaches would suggest. Narrativists share with realists and neo-positivists the goal of creating and evaluating socio-logical concepts – the difference between them is more one of what they see as the means of reaching this end than the end in itself.[10] It is likely that the student will find her- or himself adopting an eclectic approach to biographical analysis that borrows freely from all three traditions.

Appendix 1 – Analysis Exercises

As with interviewing, the practical experience of working with real data is necessary if you are to develop a grasp of coding and analysing biographical information. These analysis exercises are designed to give you experience of the several approaches to biographical data. They are intended to be done in conjunction with the interviewing exercises at the end of the previous chapter, with the material arising from those interviews providing the data for these exercises.[11] The intention of this set of exercises is to sensitize you to the different modes of analysis that the different approaches to biographical research follow. Hence, you should do all of the exercises in order to get the most out of them. While, with the exception of the group 'micro-analysis' exercise, the exercises can be done using detailed interview notes, they will be more effective if a verbatim transcript of actual verbal dialogue from an interview is used.

Exercise 1 – Concept generation

The purpose of the first exercise is to give you experience of using a grounded theory approach to analysis in order to generate concepts from an unfocused interview. This type of analysis would be used by a 'realist' or 'narrativist' during their first pass through the data after an initial, unfocused interview.

Go through the transcript of your first, unfocused, interview. Code what your respondent has said by the topics he or she is covering and the links they are making between different topics. Essentially, this first 'pass' through the data is a process of sorting and categorization. The size of the units you are coding will depend upon how often the respondent seems to change from one topic to another. The units may be single sentences or lines of text, the units sometimes could be as small as single phrases, and sometimes larger units will be appro-priate – whole paragraphs or lengthy sections of text. It is quite possible that you will discover that parts of what the respondent said seem to fall into more than one category. In such cases you will need to give a single section of text several overlapping codes. This is perfectly acceptable and may end up pointing to important conceptual links that you had not anticipated beforehand.

If you did a completely unfocused interview, in which the respondent was asked to tell the story of their life, the categories that arise from the data will be largely unpredictable and dependent upon what the respondent has chosen to talk about. If you chose to centre the interview on a specific topic in the respondent's life, you probably will have had some idea of the likely topics that the respondent will cover. In this latter case, these expected topics may affect how you code the data – you may discover yourself paying particular attention to whether what the respondent said can be placed into some of these anticipated categories. (To put it another way, your prior social science knowledge will affect how you decide to code the data.)

After the first pass through the data, look over the codings that result. Do some of the codes seem to fall into a structure of categories, perhaps with some codings appearing to be sub-headings or special cases of other codings? Try to set up some rudimentary structures of categories. Then, make a second pass through the data in which you look at the transcript in the light of these coding structures. This second pass may cause you to make some changes to your coding. You may want to add some new codings, change a code, or break down a large block of text that is under one heading into a number of smaller blocks. At the end of this second pass, re-evaluate the general structures of coding categories. (At this point, you may decide additional coding passes through the data are needed – it is up to you.)

Next, look over the coding structures that have resulted, paying particular attention to the following points:

1   Do there seem to be logical gaps in the categories that resulted from the coding; for example, things that were not mentioned by the respondent that would seem to be relevant or instances or situations that did not affect the respondent but that could arise for someone else?
2   Can you refine the existing category structure further? (a) When looked at broadly, do some categories seem to be subsets or special cases of other categories? (b) When two sets of categories overlap, is it possible that each category set is actually a special case of a broader, overarching, category?
3   Do some categories seem to be 'negatives' of other categories (that is, the opposite or absence of the other)?
4   Do there appear to be inconsistencies or areas of text that seem to contradict other areas of text?

These considerations should help you refine the category system further. In addition, the above points will help to point out gaps or ambiguities in the first interview. This will help you decide upon questions or areas that should be included in the semi-structured interview schedule that forms the basis of a second interview (which is an exercise in the previous chapter).

Turn in a transcript of the first interview, with the codings given to the sections of text indicated clearly in the margin. This transcript should be accompanied by a diagram of the structure of the categories that you developed in your coding. (The set of categories you developed may be fairly simple – especially if you only had a limited transcript based upon only ten minutes of talking time or if your respondent was not particularly communicative.) This material should be accompanied by a brief explanation of the category structure and the process by which you arrived at it.

Exercise 2 – Concept testing

The purpose of this exercise is to give you experience of the neo-positivist approach to biographical research in which pre-existing theory or concepts are evaluated in the light of empirical data. In this exercise, you will analyse the transcript of Interview 2 from the exercises at the end of the previous chapter. Interview 2 was carried out with the aid of a semi-structured interview schedule. This schedule consisted of a set of questions, probes and prompts which had been developed to 'fill in the gaps' of the category structure developed after coding Interview 1. If you have utilized a specific interview topic which has a developed body of social science theory, these questions and probes also will have been designed to tap concepts and ideas that that theory would deem significant.

As before, the interview transcript will be coded. This time, however, you will set up a preliminary category structure or coding framework *prior to looking at the transcript*. This coding framework will be developed from the category structure you had at the end of coding Interview 1 and from the semi-structured interview schedule. The coding framework will reflect the structure and organization of the theory or concepts that you are testing in Interview 2. (This 'theory' or 'body of concepts' will be either the category structure that arose during the analysis of Interview 1 and/or the social science topic that you have chosen for your interviews.) The coding framework can be thought of as the results you anticipate from Interview 2 – in effect, hypotheses about what you expect the respondent to say when questioned.

Go through the transcript, categorizing the text as before, only this time instead of working on an *ad hoc* basis, you will use the coding framework as a starting point of categorization. If text fits neatly into the coding framework, the information in the coded material should help build the theory. It may be that the text gives information that either supports or undermines an expectation that you have (that is, confirms or disconfirms a hypothesis). It also may be that new material neither clearly supports nor clearly undermines your expectations, but rather provides additional information. If this is the case, this additional information can be incorporated to refine or develop your concept structure further. Finally, it is quite possible that the respondent will talk about items that do not fit into the pre-existing coding framework at all. In that instance, you will need to develop new categories as you did in the previous concept generation exercise.

Turn in a transcript of the second interview, with the codings given to the sections of text indicated clearly in the margin. This transcript should be accompanied by 'before' and 'after' diagrams of the structure of the coding framework. The 'after' coding framework diagram should show where the alterations were made: 'new branches' added; 'old branches' deleted or modified; and sections that have been confirmed. This material should be accompanied by a report of how the information given by the respondent led to the development of the coding framework and how the person interviewed fits into the category structure that has been developed.

Exercise 3 – The narrative approach

The purpose of this exercise is to sensitize you to the issues that differentiate the narrative approach from the realist and neo-positivist approaches to biographical research. It consists of three parts.

Exercise 3a

Look at the transcripts of Interviews 1 and 2 again, only this time concentrate upon the interaction between the interviewer and interviewee. Discuss how the interaction between the interviewer (you) and the interviewee may have affected the conduct of the interview. In your discussion, consider the following points:

- Pay special attention to the places in the interview where the interviewer said something and to what the interviewee said just before and just after that point. Was the interviewer's question/ remark relatively unobtrusive in that it only had the effect of helping the interview progress? Or did the interviewer's interjection change the course of the interview by causing the interviewee to alter their train of thought or perhaps break off a fruitful line of discussion? (You should not worry if you have to admit that your questioning affected the course of the interview adversely. The point of the interviewing exercise was to gain experience in interviewing. Anyway, interviewing requires having to 'think on your feet' and respond quickly, so even experienced interviewers will make mistakes. What is important is recognizing these mistakes and learning from them.)
- What effect did the relative statuses of the interviewee and interviewer have upon the conduct of the interview? For example, if you interviewed an older member of your family, how differently do you think the interview would have gone if they had been interviewed by a stranger, or someone more their own age?
- Do you think there were particular topics that the interviewee may have avoided or skated around due to reasons such as embarrassment, lack of trust and so on?

- Did *you* as the interviewer avoid some topics for the same reasons, such as your own embarrassment, or because you expected some topics would make the interviewee uneasy?
- What are the pros and cons of interviewing someone you know? Or interviewing a stranger?

Exercise 3b

Go through the transcripts once more. This time, categorize the text by whether the interviewee is:

1 Reporting facts or events;
2 Narrating a 'story';
3 Making an assertion or argumentation.

Write a summary of the points or 'morals' of the 'stories' the interviewee told and the points of the arguments or assertions they made. Does this summary broadly coincide or conflict with the conceptual structure that you developed in the previous exercises? Do you think that the approach of the previous exercises is artificial – that it breaks down the coherent whole of the interviewee's narration into atomized bits?

Exercise 3c

Give the person you interviewed copies of the transcripts of both interviews with the codings attached, a copy of the report you wrote about Interview 2 which includes your view of how they fit into the category structure that has been developed, and your report for Exercise 3b. After they have had time to look over the material, discuss with them how they feel about what you made of their interviews. Turn in a report of that discussion. The following may be points that could arise:

- Do they want to change the transcripts? Why is this? Is it because they want to 'edit' the grammar? Do they disagree about reported facts or what they said? Are they having second thoughts about 'having said too much' ?
- Do they see the coding framework you developed as reasonable?
- Did you feel uneasy about showing them the results of your analysis of their interviews? Did knowing they were going to see your analysis results cause you to alter or 'self-censor' what you wrote? If they criticized your analysis, how did you react?

Micro-analysis group exercise

(This exercise should be undertaken by a small group of, say, 4–8 people working together for one hour. Each person is given a copy of the same transcript passage.) Conduct a 'micro-analysis' of a short segment of transcript chosen because it is a significant or interesting point drawn from a larger interview. (Twenty lines should be more than enough – you will be lucky if you can cover ten lines in an hour.)

Look at *only* the first sentence or major clause in the text. 'Brainstorm' about all possible reasonable interpretations (hypotheses) that one could draw from that single unit. These interpretations should include how the interviewee may be reacting to the interviewer or to the way questions are being phrased. One person should act as 'secretary', noting down all the interpretations the group comes up with.

Move on to the second sentence or major clause. Can some of the interpretations/hypotheses that arose from the first unit of text be ruled out by this second unit? Looking at the two text units together, 'brainstorm' to see whether additional hypotheses can be proposed.

Then, move on to the third text unit and repeat the procedure. The group should go through this sequence until the end of the passage or the allotted time is reached. At the end of the exercise, consider the final list of interpretations/hypotheses. Was 'saturation' reached where no new interpretations were being generated? Did the exercise produce a more in-depth understanding of the levels of the text beyond that which one person could have reached with an attentive reading?

Appendix 2 – Computer Programs for Qualitative Data Analysis

Starting at the beginning of the 1980s, an innovation in social science research has been the introduction of computer programs designed to analyse qualitative data. While the rate of their uptake has been accelerating, their adoption is by no means universal. The current situation among qualitative researchers is similar to that for the use of the internet among social scientists about five years ago or for the use of word processors a decade before then – a vocal minority has become skilled in the new technology and loudly proselytizes its benefits, a middle group accepts that there may be benefits to the innovation but are ambivalent about whether they have the time, resources or aptitude to take it up, and another minority believes that computerization has no place to play in qualitative social science. Much of the ambivalence and hostility stems from misconceptions about what computerized qualitative data analysis entails.

Computer programs designed to analyse qualitative data were developed by qualitative researchers. Their genesis began when qualitative researchers began to use word processors to type up their transcripts and notes. Once qualitative material was typed into a word processor file, it in effect was computerized. Some people quickly realized that some of the functions available with word processors could be used as aids to a qualitative analysis. For instance, a 'Find' function could be used to locate the occurrences of a word or phrase in a lengthy transcript – thereby making it easier to locate a useful quote or the spot where an interviewee had been talking about a topic of interest. As aids to analysis, blocks of text could be highlighted, extracted into a separate file or moved into juxtaposition with another block of text on the same topic. From there, it was only a small step to writing special computation routines to carry out purpose-built manipulations of text, and the first qualitative data analysis computer programs were born.

Qualitative data analysis programs have been developed by qualitative researchers and the functions they perform duplicate procedures that qualitative researchers previously had been doing by hand. The main difference is not that the qualitative analyst using a computer program carries out new or different procedures but rather that he or she carries out the same or analogous procedures to those that used to be done by hand, only much more quickly and reliably. Starting with the most simple procedures and working up, let us consider what qualitative data analysis programs can do:

1. Locate individual words or phrases.   As mentioned above, the ability to find all or the next occurrence of a word or phrase in a lengthy transcript can be extremely useful. For instance, the author wanted to locate each point where William had mentioned his brother who had had a mental breakdown. One way of locating these points was to have the computer program search each transcript for all occurrences of the brother's name. This is not foolproof (William sometimes talked about the brother without naming him), but it did immediately turn up several instances where the brother had been mentioned.

2. Speed up coding.   One of the first steps a qualitative researcher is likely to follow in an analysis is to go through the transcript and code portions of text, either generating the coding scheme 'on the fly' or coding into a pre-existing scheme. If done manually, this usually involves writing notes in the margin next to the transcript. If a single block of text needs to be given several codes, the marginal notes can become quite complex.

An analyst using a qualitative data analysis program does the equivalent by going through the text on screen and highlighting the portions of text they wish to attach a certain code to. The program records this coding and can easily deal with multiple or overlapping codings being attached to the same block of text. If an analyst is using grounded theory procedures to generate a coding scheme as they work their way through a transcript, the computerized approach is clearly superior. The program will allow the researcher to view a diagram or summary of the codes generated so far, thereby making the generation of *ad hoc* codes a much more rational and controlled process.

3. View coding results. Once a transcript has been coded, a manual analyst often makes a photocopy of the transcript and then cuts up the copy in order to sort the text into the coded categories. Care must be taken to preserve the original line numbers of each block of text so that its placement in the complete transcript is not lost. If a block of text is coded into more than one category, more than one copy must be made.

An analyst using a computerized program can do the equivalent by retrieving all the blocks of text that have been assigned a code. The original placement in the transcript or other codes given to all or part of the same text block are not affected.

4. Retrieving logical combinations of codings. Qualitative analysis programs allow the analyst to locate blocks of text whose codings match some logical combination. For instance, two codes given to William's interviews were 'Sports/Running' and 'Business connections'. Instances where William spoke about business connections he had made through his sports activities could be found by retrieving those blocks of text where these two codes overlapped.

In theory, these types of logical retrieval can be done manually as well. For instance, one could have sorted through all of the 'Sports/ Running' text manually in order to find any blocks of text that also had a 'Business connections' code written in their margin. In practice, the tedium and time required to do this (which a computer program can do virtually in an instant) means that a researcher working manually will keep their retrievals to a minimum.

As well as doing retrievals with little effort on the analyst's part, computer programs also have the capacity to carry out extremely complex retrievals. These more elaborate routines for carrying out complex retrievals can be very specialized and clever indeed. (For instance, carrying out a retrieval to locate the *next* time a text block occurs *after* another coding appears in the transcript.)

5. Writing notes and 'memos'. Qualitative analysts often will write themselves notes or 'memos' about procedures they have followed or ideas that occur to them while working with the data. Qualitative analysis programs cater to this by allowing the researcher to attach such notes or memos directly to the transcript or to coding categories.

6. Keeping a record of all stages in an analysis. When an analyst is working with qualitative data using a computer, the program will keep track of operations as they are performed, automatically recording the date and time they took place. This allows researchers at a later date to retrace the steps taken in the analysis. For instance, he/she will be able to tell when a coding category was first created, whether it was modified afterwards, when a note or memo was written and so on.

Note that qualitative data programs also have some limited capacity for quantitative procedures. They will generate some basic numerical information about the transcript, such as the percentage of the text that is coded into a given category, and some have the capacity to export quantitative information to statistical analysis packages. These functions, however, come about largely as a by-product of the primary qualitative analysis functions. It would be a gross misconception to see qualitative data analysis packages as designed to quantify or routinize the analysis of qualitative information.

There is a steep 'learning curve' with qualitative data analysis programs, particularly since many qualitative researchers will have had little exposure to computing outside of using e-mail and their word processor. Until the user actually has coded some data, given it at least a rudimentary coding scheme, and retrieved some text using the codes, the use of these programs can be confusing. Once the initial confusion is over, however, you should be able to work with your chosen program with increasing efficiency as you gain experience. Anyone intending to do anything more than only a very small amount of work with qualitative data is advised in the strongest terms to learn to use one of these extremely valuable aids to the analyst.

Notes

[1] This observation should be seen as only a very general rule of thumb. The classic participant observation studies stretched over years and a lengthy series of in-depth interviews can require many hours of a researcher's personal involvement. In the same vein, the quantitative researcher who has completed a long and tedious statistical analysis of a complex dataset will not appreciate being told that statistical analyses are quick and easy. Nevertheless, the amount of labour necessary to carry out the collection of the thousands of quantitative interviews associated with a large survey is massive and can be contrasted with the relative speed of a modern-day statistical analysis that will process the resulting data. The basic point is that students often fail to realize the amount of effort and difficulty associated with a qualitative analysis.

[2] In the sense of repeating the same questions to new respondents just like those interviewed up to that point.

[3] He is correct and his perception would be confirmed by quantitative data on social mobility and changes in the occupational structure of Northern Ireland across the century.

[4] The 'Hawthorne effect' refers to a famous series of studies in the sociology of work that took place during the late 1920s at the Western Electric plant located in Hawthorne, New Jersey. The researchers

gradually came to the realization that a major cause of changes in the workers' performance was that they knew they were being observed. The term 'Hawthorne effect' has come to stand generally for researcher-induced effects caused by the subjects being aware that they are objects of study.

[5] In sub-atomic physics, many of the phenomena are so delicate that any measurement will profoundly interfere with the phenomenon one is attempting to record. By extension to social research, one must question in an interview to get a respondent to tell about their views, but this questioning will affect what they tell and how they tell it.

[6] The purpose of this example is to demonstrate in an exaggerated manner that the narrative approach does not discount constraints imposed by an individual's situation in social structure and networks. The example should not be taken as implying that the realist or neo-positivist approaches would fail to appreciate that these three individuals are quite different.

[7] Even if the person could recall the whole of their life.

[8] This assertion, that one can build upon the results of a thematic analysis that explains the perspective of the respondent *in the present* in order to reach conclusions about the viewpoints the respondent may have held *in the past*, is controversial and open to considerable doubt. Unless one has in-depth qualitative data collected in the past – in effect, a longitudinal study – the assertion cannot be evaluated empirically.

[9] Note that in the narrative approach even deliberate falsification – lying – becomes just more grist to the analyst's mill. If a respondent is lying, the analyst can concentrate upon questions such as why the respondent has chosen to lie and what form the falsification has taken. For instance, the author once carried out an interview in which the respondent gave an elaborate account of their job as an assistant manager working the 'graveyard shift' (12 midnight to 8 am) in a retail store. The only problem was that the store maintained normal daytime hours and was closed between 9pm and 8:30am. The respondent was unemployed and had chosen a story that could fit with his everyday living pattern of late rising and not being at work during the day and early evening as well as give him a white-collar status.

[10] As discussed in Chapter 1, researchers tend to be pragmatic in their work, applying techniques because of their practical utility rather than because they feel they must conform to the tenets of some methodological 'church'. They, and the student, are under no compulsion to limit themselves to the insights of only one approach.

[11] As an alternative to using data from interviews of your own, your instructor may choose to provide interview transcripts for analysis.

6

The Biographical Perspective

CONTENTS

This text has been structured by three approaches to biographical research: a realist approach that uses inductive grounded theory techniques to build theory; a neo-positivist approach that adopts the more traditional perspective of deductive theory-testing; and a narrativist approach that concentrates upon the construction of viewpoints of reality that are shared between the interviewee and their interrogator. Each of these three approaches has been shown to lead to differing approaches to the collection and analysis of biographical information. It has been the position of this text that each of these approaches benefits greatly from a more rigorous consideration of the theorisation of time – sociological views of ageing, cohort, generation, and period and historical effects, including concepts developed by quantitative social scientists. Finally, even in these 'postmodern', 'post-industrialized' times, families continue to exert seminal effects upon people's life histories and the life stories that they will tell, so that the collection of family histories and social genealogies overlap with biographical research to the extent that the methods are synonymous.

A paradox provides the crucial tension that underlies present-day biographical research. Biographical methods have enjoyed a renaissance in recent decades so that at the turn of the millennium 'the biographical perspective' constitutes a truly international corpus of multidisciplinary research. Popularity has bred division. Taken in their pure forms, the three approaches to biographical research embody mutually contradictory methodological standpoints. While this methodological tension between the approaches is always present and does flare up from time to time (for example, Bertaux 1996) and the replies of Fischer-Rosenthal and Rosenthal (1997) and Kochuyt (1997)), it is largely unacknowledged. At the same time, in their practice, biographical researchers tend to be eclectic and pragmatically apply the insights of each approach on a utilitarian basis. This leads to a blurring of the distinctions between the approaches. 'Realists' and 'neo-positivists' are quite aware of the dynamics of interactions between the researcher and the researched that form the central concern of the narrativist approach and will take account of them in their collection and analysis of biographical information. The ways in which narrativists deal with the development or testing of concepts in practical terms is almost indistinguishable from the methods used by realists and neo-positivists. This is the paradox: what appear as fundamental differences in approach are, in practice, largely unacknowledged and apparently have little effect on day-to-day research practice. Whether this state of affairs is healthy, and whether it can persist, are both issues that are open to debate.

Beyond the differing methodological approaches to biographical research, however, there are now glimmerings of a developing biographical perspective that could provide an overarching principle that unifies the approaches. 'This conception, whose developments are still in progress, is based on the evidence that biography is not a mere sociological product or research tool; it is primarily a social phenomenon that must be seen as a fundamental constituent of sociality' (Chanfrault-Duchet, 1995: 212). Social science tends to provide dichotomous viewpoints of reality – subjective/objective, individual/group, actor/ structure, primary/secondary. The serious adoption of a biographical perspective moves beyond this. An individual's personal biography can only be conceived of in terms that transcend his/her personal state. As people live their lives, they continuously are doing 'biographical work'; that is, as they move through life they must construct and reconstruct their self-view in response to an ever-changing society. 'Biographical work – both of individuals and through the establishing of biographical patterns in institutions[1] – is the symbolic process by which individuals achieve this balance by reflexively structuring their experiences and activities. It enables them to practically orient themselves, while dealing with events ongoingly as they go through life' (Fischer-Rosenthal, 1995: 261). In effect, in a (post)modern society, each person is compelled to be their own 'lay sociologist', siting themselves within evolving social structures.

Hence, *if* it is the case that, before an interview ever takes place, each person already has a nascent biography in place, the first task of a biographical researcher then becomes one of extracting that biography in as intact and unsullied a state as possible. Particularly for 'narrativists', the preferred method is unfocused interviewing and non-directive questioning. The interviewee has a working biography that will form the initial 'data' upon which biographical analysis is based. 'The aim of reconstructing a biography [during an unfocussed interview] is thus to discover the principles along which life histories and life stories are built in specific social and personal relations as well as in specific time and interactional contexts' (Breckner, 1998: 3). This is a central insight of the narrative approach.

In terms of social structure, within the biographical perspective the individual is located in social networks both of origin and of current position – networks, for instance, of family (both the family of origin and the present family), of work position/employment structure (and job history), of one's personal life course as contrasted to and evaluated by the wider societal historical events that have taken place during the lifetime, and so on. Furthermore, adopting the biographical perspective implies taking a different view of time. Non-biographical social research maintains the fiction of 'an eternal present'. While people have a past and (probably) a future, the researcher's only point of real interest is the present – present attitudes and motivations, present activities, present situations and placements and so on. In contrast, if a biographical perspective is adopted by the researcher, the present moment must be located within a time span that begins at least with the individual's birth (and probably earlier), extends to the present and (because one's evaluation of present situation includes anticipations of future developments) also stretches into the future. 'Biographies are global constructions by which individuals constitute a defined present within the specific horizons of the past (retentions) and the future (protentions)' (Bertaux and Kohli, 1984: 222). Barriers of self/society and present/past/future become transparent in the biographical perspective. Rather than being merely (one of a choice of three) approaches to collecting and analysing biographical data, the adoption of a genuine biographical *perspective* implies a sociological position that has the potential for transcending some of the constraints of sociological analysis (Chanfrault-Duchet, 1995: 212–15). It is this transcendent quality that gives the developing biographical perspective its true significance.

> Duke Senior: *Thou seest we are not all alone unhappy:*
> *This wide and universal theatre*
> *Presents more woeful pageants than the scene*
> *Wherein we play in.*
> Jaques: *All the world's a stage,*
> *And all the men and women merely players:*
> *They have their exits and their entrances;*
> *And one man in his time plays many parts,*
> *His acts being seven ages. At first the infant,*
> *Mewling and puking in the nurse's arms.*
> *And then the whining school-boy, with his satchel*
> *And shining morning face, creeping like snail*
> *Unwillingly to school. And then the lover,*
> *Sighing like furnace, with a woeful ballad*
> *Made to his mistress' eyebrow. Then a soldier,*
> *Full of strange oaths and bearded like the pard,*
> *Jealous in honour, sudden and quick in quarrel,*
> *Seeking the bubble reputation*
> *Even in the cannon's mouth. And then the justice,*
> *In fair round belly with good capon lined,*
> *With eyes severe and beard of formal cut,*
> *Full of wise saws and modern instances;*
> *And so he plays his part. The sixth age shifts*
> *Into the lean and slipper'd pantaloon,*
> *With spectacles on nose and pouch on side,*
> *His youthful hose, well saved, a world too wide*
> *For his shrunk shank; and his big manly voice,*
> *Turning again toward childish treble, pipes*

And whistles in his sound. Last scene of all,
That ends this strange eventful history,
Is second childishness and mere oblivion,
Sans teeth, sans eyes, sans taste, sans everything.

William Shakespeare, *As You Like It*, Act 2, Scene 7

Note

[1] This need to carry out 'biographical work', the ongoing reconstruction of identity in response to changing situations, could apply just as well at levels above that of the individual, such as the evolving identities of organizations, institutions, ethnic groups or even nations.

REFERENCES

Alheit, Peter (1994) 'Everyday Time and Life Time: On the problems of healing contradictory experiences of time', *Time & Society*, 3 (3): 305–19.

Andorka, Rudolf (1997) 'Social Mobility in Hungary since the Second World War: Interpretations through surveys and through family histories', in D. Bertaux and P. Thompson (eds), *Pathways to Social Class: A qualitative approach to social mobility.* Oxford: Clarendon Press. 259–98.

Arensberg, Conrad M. and Kimball, Solon T. (1968) *Family and Community in Ireland.* Cambridge, Mass.: Harvard University Press.

Atkinson, Robert (1998) *The Life Story Interview.* Vol. 44, *Qualitative Research Methods.* Thousand Oaks, CA: Sage.

Becker, Howard S. (1970) 'The Relevance of Life Histories', in N.K. Denzin (ed.), *Sociological Methods: A sourcebook.* New York: McGraw-Hill Book Company. 419–28.

Bertaux, D. (1974) 'On the Necessity of an Historical Framework for the Understanding of Social Phenomena: The case of anthrodistribution', paper presented to the International Sociological Association Research Committee on Social Stratification and Mobility, Toronto.

Bertaux, Daniel (ed.) (1981) *Biography and Society: The life history approach in the social sciences.* London: Sage.

Bertaux, Daniel (1991b) 'From Methodological Monopoly to Pluralism in the Sociology of Social Mobility', in S. Dex (ed.), *Life and Work History Analyses: Qualitative and quantitative developments.* London: Routledge. 73–92.

Bertaux, Daniel (1995) 'Social Genealogies Commented On and Compared: An instrument for observing social mobility in "the *Longue Durée*" ', *Current Sociology*, 43 (2/3): 69–88.

Bertaux, Daniel (1996) 'A Response to Thierry Kochuyt's "Biographical and Empiricist Illusions: A reply to recent criticism" ', *Biography & Society Newsletter*, December: 2–6.

Bertaux, Daniel (1997) 'Transmission in Extreme Situations: Russian families expropriated by the October Revolution', in D. Bertaux and

P. Thompson (eds), *Pathways to Social Class: A qualitative approach to social mobility.* Oxford: Clarendon Press.

Bertaux, Daniel and Bertaux-Wiame, Isabelle (1981a) 'Artisanal Bakery in France: How it lives and why it survives', in F. Bechhofer and B. Elliott (eds), *The Petite Bourgeoisie: Comparative studies of an uneasy stratum.* London: Macmillan Press. 155–81.

Bertaux, Daniel and Bertaux-Wiame, Isabelle (1981b) 'Life Stories in the Bakers' Trade', in D. Bertaux (ed.), *Biography and Society: The life history approach in the social sciences.* London: Sage. 169–90.

Bertaux, Daniel and Bertaux-Wiame, Isabelle (1997) 'Heritage and its Lineage: A case history of transmission and social mobility over five generations', in D. Bertaux and P. Thompson (eds), *Pathways to Social Class: A qualitative approach to social mobility.* Oxford: Clarendon Press. 62–97.

Bertaux, Daniel and Kohli, Martin (1984) 'The Life Story Approach: A continental view', *Annual Review of Sociology,* 10: 215–37.

Bertaux, Daniel and Thompson, Paul (eds) (1993) *Between Generations: Family models, myths and memories.* Vol. 2, *International Yearbook of Oral History and Life Stories.* Oxford: Oxford University Press.

Bertaux, Daniel and Thompson, P. (eds) (1997) *Pathways to Social Class: A qualitative approach to social mobility.* Oxford: Clarendon Press.

Bertaux-Wiame, Isabelle (1993) 'The Pull of Family Ties: Intergenerational relationships and life paths', in D. Bertaux and P. Thompson (eds), *Between Generations: Family models, myths, and memories.* Vol. 2, *International Yearbook of Oral History and Life Stories.* Oxford: Oxford University Press. 39–50.

Breckner, Roswitha (1998) 'Just Single Cases? Procedures and methodological arguments for hermeneutic case analysis', paper presented at the conference, 'Biographical Methods in the Social Sciences', Tavistock Clinic, London.

Brose, H.-G. (1986) 'Lebenszeit und biographishce Zeitperspektive im Kontext sozialer Zeitstrukturen', in F. Furstenburg and I. Mörth (eds), *Zeit als Strukurelement von Lebenswelt und Gesellschaft.* Linz: Trauner. 175–207.

Chanfrault-Duchet, Marie-Francoise (1991) 'Narrative Structures, Social Models, and Symbolic Representation in the Life Story', in S. Berger Gluck and D. Patai (eds), *Women's Words: The feminist practice of oral history.* London: Routledge. 77–92.

Chanfrault-Duchet, Marie-Francoise (1995) 'Biographical Research in Former West Germany', *Current Sociology,* 43 (2/3): 209–19.

Chanlasinski, Józef (1991) 'The Life Records of the Young Generation of Polish Peasants as a Manifestation of Contemporary Culture', in D. Bertaux (ed.), *Biography and Society: The Life history approach in the social sciences.* London: Sage.

Chase, S.E. (1995) 'Taking Narrative Seriously: Consequences for method and theory in interview studies', in R. Josselson and A. Liebich (eds), *The Narrative Study of Lives, Vol. 1: Interpreting Experience.* Thousand Oaks, CA: Sage. 1–26.

Cook, Judith A. and Fonow, Mary Margaret (1990) 'Knowledge and Women's Interests: Issues of epistemology and methodology in feminist sociological research', in J. McCarl Nielsen (ed.), *Feminist Research Methods*. Boulder: Westview Press. 69–93.

Corbin, Juliet and Anselm Strauss (1990) 'Grounded Theory Research: Procedures, canons, and evaluative criteria', *Qualitative Sociology*, 13 (1): 3–21.

Davis, Kathy (1997) ' "Imagined Communities"? Some Reflections on Biographical Research', *Biography & Society Newsletter*, December: 2–5.

Denzin, Norman K. (1995) 'Stanley and Clifford: Undoing an interactionist text', *Current Sociology*, 43 (2/3): 115–23.

Dex, Shirley (1990) 'Goldthorpe on Class and Gender: The case against', in J. Clark, C. Modgil and S. Modgil (eds), *John H. Goldthorpe: Consensus and controversy*. London: The Falmer Press. 135–52.

Easterlin, R.A. (1978) *Birth and Fortune: The impact of numbers on personal welfare*. New York: Basic Books.

Eisenstadt, S.N. (1956) *From Generation to Generation: Age groups and social structure*. Glencoe, Illinois: Free Press.

Elder, G.H., Jr. (1974) *Children of the Great Depression: Social change in life experience*. Chicago: University of Chicago Press.

Elder, G.H., Jr. and Rockwell, R.C. (1979) 'Economic Depression and Postwar Opportunity in Men's Lives: A study of life patterns and mental health', in R.G. Simmons (ed.), *Research in Community and Mental Health*, Vol. 1. Greenwich, Connecticut: JAI Press. 249–303.

Elliott, Brian (1997) 'Migration, Mobility, and Social Process: Scottish migrants in Canada', in D. Bertaux and P. Thompson (eds), *Pathways to Social Class: A qualitative approach to social mobility*. Oxford: Clarendon Press. 198–229.

Erikson, R., König, W., Lüttinger, P. and Müller, W. (1988) *CASMIN International Mobility Superfile: Documentation*. Mannheim: Institut für Sozialwissenschaften, Universität Mannheim.

Fielding, Nigel (1993) 'Qualitative Interviewing', in N. Gilbert (ed.), *Researching Social Life*. London: Sage. 135–53.

Fischer, Wolfgang and Kohli, Martin (1987) 'Biographieforschung', in W. Voges (ed.), *Methoden der Biographie–und Lebenlaufforschung*. Opladen: Leske & Budrich. 25–49.

Fischer, Wolfgang, Fuchs, W. and Jinnecker, J. (1985) *Jugendliche und Erwachsene '85. Generationen im Vergleich. Shell-Jugendstudie*, 5 Vols. Opladen: Leske & Budrich.

Fischer-Rosenthal, Wolfram (1995) 'The Problem with Identity: Biography as solution to some (post)-modernist dilemmas', *Comenius*, 15: 250–65.

Fischer-Rosenthal, Wolfram and Rosenthal, Gabrielle (1997) 'Daniel Bertaux's Complaints or Against False Dichotomies in Biographical Research', *Biography & Society Newsletter*, December 1997: 5–11.

Giele, Janet Z. and Elder, Glen H., Jr. (1998) 'Life Course Research: Development of a field', in J.Z. Giele and G.H. Elder, Jr. (eds),

Methods of Life Course Research: Qualitative and quantitative approaches. Thousand Oaks, CA: Sage. 5–27

Goldthorpe, J.H. (1985) 'On Economic Development and Social Mobility', *British Journal of Sociology,* 36: 549–73.

Hayes, Bernadette C. and Miller, Robert L. (1993) 'The Silenced Voice: Female social mobility patterns with particular reference to the British Isles', *British Journal of Sociology,* 44 (4): 535–41.

Heritage, John (1997) 'Conversation Analysis and Institutional Talk: Analyzing data', in David Silverman (ed.), *Qualitative Research: Theory, method and practice.* London: Sage. 161–82 and 254.

Holloway, Wendy and Jefferson, Tony (1997) 'Eliciting Narrative Through the In-Depth Interview', *Qualitative Inquiry,* 3 (1): 53–70.

Holstein, J.A. and J.F. Gubrium (1995) *The Active Interview.* Sage Qualitative Research Methods Series 37. Thousand Oaks, CA: Sage.

Holstein, J.A. and J.F. Gubrium (1997) 'Active Interviewing', in D. Silverman (ed.), *Qualitative Research: Theory, method and practice.* London: Sage. 113–129.

Jackson, John A. (1977) 'The Irish Occupational Index: A new scale for coding Irish occupational data', paper presented at meeting of the International Sociological Association Research Committee on Social Stratification and Mobility, Dublin.

Jackson, John A. and Miller, Robert L. (1983) 'Who Gets the Farm? Birth Order and Family Size in Two Irish Populations', paper presented to the International Sociological Association Research Committee on Social Stratification and Mobility, Amsterdam.

Jackson, John A. and Eoin O'Sullivan (1993) 'Family Genealogies', paper presented to International Sociological Association Research Committee on Social Stratification and Mobility, Trondheim, Norway, 20–22 May.

Josselson, Ruthellen (1995) 'Imagining the Real: Empathy, narrative and the dialogic self', in R. Josselson and A. Lieblich (eds), *Interpreting Experience.* Vol. 3, *The Narrative Study of Lives.* Thousand Oaks, CA: Sage. 27–44.

Kallmeyer, W. and Schütze, F. (1977) 'Zur Konstitution von Kommunikationsschemata', in D. Wegner (ed.), *Gesprächsanalyse.* Hamburg: Buske. 159–274.

Kertzer, D.I. (1983) 'Generation As a Sociological Problem', *Annual Review of Sociology,* 9: 125–49.

Kochuyt, Thierry (1997) 'Could Objective Realities Tell Us a Story? Reply to Bertaux', *Biography & Society Newsletter,* December 1997: 11–15.

Kohli, Martin (1981) 'Biography: Account, text, method', in D. Bertaux (ed.), *Biography and Society: The life history approach in the social sciences.* London: Sage.

Kohli, Martin (1985) 'Die Institutionalisierung des Lebenslaufs', *Kölner Zeitschrift für Soziologie und Sozialpsychologie,* 37 (1): 1–29.

Kohli, Martin (1986a) 'Biographical Research in the German Language Area', in Zygmunt Dulczewski (ed.), *A Commemorative Book in Honor of Florian Znaniecki on the Centenary of His Birth*. Poznan: Uniwersytet im. Adama Mickiewicza w Poznaniu. 9–10.

Kohli, Martin (1986b) 'Social Organisation and Subjective Construction of the Life Course', in A.B. Sorenson, F.E. Weinert and L.R. Sherrod (eds), *Human Development and the Life Course: Multidisciplinary perspectives*. Hillsdale, New Jersey and London: Lawrence Erlbaum Associates. 271–92.

Kohli, Martin (1988) 'Normalbiographie und Individualität: zur institutionellen Dynamik des gegenwärtigen Lebenslaufregimes', in H.-G. Brose and B. Hildenbrand (eds), *Vom Ende des Individuums zur Individualität ohne Ende*. Opladen: Leske & Budrich. 33–53.

König, W., Lüttinger, P. and Müller, W. (1987) 'A Comparative Analysis of the Development and Structure of Educational Systems – Methodological Foundations and the Construction of a Comparative Educational Scale', CASMIN Working Paper No. 12. Mannheim: Institut für Sozialwissenschaften, Universität Mannheim.

Kontula, Osmo and Haavia-Mannila, Elivia (1995) *Sexual Pleasures: Enhancement of Sex Life in Finland, 1971–1992*. Aldershot: Dartmouth.

Labov, W. (1972) 'The Transformation of Experience in Narrative Syntax', in W. Labov (ed.), *Language in the Inner City: Studies in the black English vernacular*. Philadelphia: University of Pennsylvania Press. 354–96.

Labov, W. (1982) 'Speech Actions and Reactions in Personal Narrative', in D. Tannen (ed.), *Analyzing Discourse: Text and talk*. Washington, D.C.: Georgetown University Press. 219–47.

Labov, W. and Waletzky, J. (1967) 'Narrative Analysis: Oral versions of personal experience', in J. Helm (ed.), *Essays on the Verbal and Visual Arts*. Seattle: University of Washington Press. 12–44.

Lang, Alice Beatriz da Sliva Gordo (1998) 'Family History and Identity in São Paulo', Paper presented at the XIVth World Congress of Sociology, Montreal.

Laufer, R. and Bengtson, V. (1974) 'Generations, Aging and Social Stratification: On the development of generation units', *Journal of Social Issues*, 30: 181–203.

Lee, Everett S. (1966) 'A Theory of Migration', *Demography*, 3: 47–57.

Lee, R.M. (1994) *Mixed and Matched Interreligious Courtship and Marriage in Northern Ireland*. Vol. 2, *Class, Ethnicity, Gender and the Democratic Nation*. London: University Press of America.

Lewis, Oscar (1970) *Anthropological Essays*. New York: Random House.

Madge, John (1962) *The Origins of Scientific Sociology*. London: Tavistock Publications.

Mannheim, K. (1952) 'The Problem of Generations', in P. Keczekemeti (ed.), *Essays on the Sociology of Knowledge*. New York: Oxford University Press.

Marias, J. (1970) *Generations: A historical method*. Birmingham: University of Alabama Press.

McRae, Susan (1990) 'Women and Class Analysis', in J. Clark, C.

Modgil and S. Modgil (eds), *John H. Goldthorpe: Consensus and controversy.* London: The Falmer Press. 117–34.

Miller, Robert L. (1998) 'The Limited Concerns of Social Mobility Research', *Current Sociology,* 46 (4): 145–63.

Miller, Robert, Osborne, Robert, Cormack, Robert and Curry, Carol (1993) 'Higher Education and Labour Market Entry: The differing experiences of Northern Irish Protestants and Catholics', in R. Osborne, R. Cormack and A. Gallagher (eds), *After the Reforms: Education and policy in Northern Ireland.* Aldershot: Avebury. 255–82.

Miller, Robert, Wilford, Rick and Donoghue, Freda (1996) *Women and Political Participation in Northern Ireland.* Aldershot: Avebury.

Mills, C. Wright (1959) *The Sociological Imagination.* New York: Oxford University Press

Muxel, Anne (1993) 'Family Memory: A review of French works on the subject', in D. Bertaux, and P. Thompson (eds), *Between Generations: Family models, myths and memories.* Vol. 2, *International Yearbook of Oral History and Life Stories.* Oxford: Oxford University Press. 191–7.

Myrdal, Gunnar (1944) *An American Dilemma: The Negro problem and modern democracy.* New York: Harper and Brothers.

Oakley, Ann (1981) 'Interviewing Women: A contradiction in terms', in H. Roberts (ed.), *Doing Feminist Research Methods.* London: Routledge. 30–61.

Passerini, Luisa (ed.) (1992) *Memory and Totalitarianism.* Vol. I, *International Yearbook of Oral History and Life Stories.* Oxford: Oxford University Press.

Payne, Geoff (1987) *Mobility and Change in Modern Society.* Houndsmills, Basingstoke: Macmillan.

Payne, Geoff and Abbott, Pamela (eds) (1990) *The Social Mobility of Women: Beyond male mobility models.* London: The Falmer Press.

Pilcher, J. (1994) 'Mannheim's Sociology of Generations: An under valued legacy', *British Journal of Sociology,* 45: 481–495.

Pilcher, J. (1995) *Age and Generation in Modern Britain.* Oxford: Oxford University Press.

Plummer, Ken (1983) *Documents of Life.* London: George Allen & Unwin.

Prandy, Ken and Wendy Bottero (n.d.) 'Family, Occupation and Social Stratification: 1840 to the present', Cambridge: Sociological Research Group, University of Cambridge.

Psathas, George (1995) *Conversation Analysis: The study of talk-in-interaction.* Vol. 35, *Qualitative Research Methods.* Thousand Oaks, CA: Sage.

Rammstedt, Angela (1995) 'Biographical Research in Italy', *Current Sociology,* 43 (2/3): 179–207.

Reinharz, Shulamit (1992) *Feminist Methods in Social Research.* Oxford: Oxford University Press.

Riessman, Catherine Kohler (1990) *Divorce Talk.* New Brunswick: Rutgers University Press.

Reissman, Catherine Kohler (1993) *Narrative Analysis*. Vol. 30, *Qualitative Research Methods*. Newbury Park: Sage.

Renn, H. (1987) 'Lebenslauf-Lebenszeit-Kohortenanalyse. Möglichkeiten und Grenzen eines Forshungsansatzes', in W. Voges (ed.), *Methoden der Biographie-und Lebenslaufforschung*. Opladen: Leske & Budrich.

Riley, M.W. (1973) 'Aging and Cohort Succession: Interpretations and misinterpretation', *Public Opinion Quarterly* 37: 35–9.

Riley, M.W. (1984) 'Women, Men, and the Lengthening Life Course', in A.S. Rossi (ed.), *Gender and the Life Course*. Hawthorne, N.Y.: Aldine. 333–48.

Riley, M.W. (1986) 'Overview and Highlights of a Sociological Perspective', in A.B. Sorenson, F.E. Weinert and L.R. Sherrod (eds), *Human Development and the Life Course: Multidisciplinary perspectives*. Hillsdale, New Jersey and London: Lawrence Erlbaum Associates. 153–76.

Riley, M.W. (1998) 'A Life Course Approach: Autobiographical notes', in J.Z. Giele and G.H. Elder, Jr. (eds), *Methods of Life Course Research: Qualitative and quantitative approaches*. Thousand Oaks, CA: Sage. 28–51.

Riley, M.W., Foner, A. and Waring J. (1988) 'Sociology of Age', in N.J. Smelser (ed.), *Handbook of Sociology*. Newbury Park: Sage.

Riley, M.W., Johnson, M. and Foner, A. (1972) *Aging and Society Volume III: A sociology of age stratification*. New York: Russell Sage Foundation.

Rindfleisch, A. (1994) 'Cohort Generational Influences of Consumer Socialization', *Advances in Consumer Research*, 21: 470–6.

Rosenthal, Gabriele (1990) 'The Structure and "Gestalt" of Autobiographies and its Methodological Consequences', paper presented at the Twelfth World Congress of Sociology, Madrid, Spain.

Rosenthal, Gabriele (1991) 'German War Memories: Narrability and the biographical and social functions of remembering', *Oral History* 19 (2): 34–41.

Rosenthal, Gabriele (1993) 'Reconstruction of Life Stories: Principles of selection in generating stories for narrative biographical interviews', in R. Josselson and A. Lieblich (eds), *The Narrative Study of Lives*, Vol. 1. London: Sage. 59–91.

Rosenthal, Gabriele and Bar-On, Daniel (1992) 'A Biographical Case Study of a Victimizer's Daughter's Strategy: Pseudo-identification with the victims of the Holocaust', *Journal of Narrative and Life History*, 2 (2): 105–127.

Ryder, N.B. (1965) 'The Cohort as a Concept in the Study of Social Change', *American Sociological Review*, 30: 843–61.

Schatzman, L. and Strauss, A. (1973) *Field Research*. Englewood Cliffs, New Jersey: Prentice-Hall, Inc.

Schumann, H. and Scott, J. (1989) 'Generations and Collective Memories', *American Sociological Review* 54: 359–81.

Schütze, F. (1981) 'Prozesstrukturen des Lebensablaufs', in J. Matthes, A. Preifenberger and M. Stossberg (eds), *Biographie in handlungs-wissenschaftlicher Perspektive*. Nürnberg: Verlang der Nürnberger Forschungsvereinigung e. V. 67–156.

Shaw, C.R. (1966) *The Jack Roller: A delinquent boy's own story*. Chicago: University of Chicago Press (originally published 1930).

Silverman, David and Jaber, F. Gubrium (1994) 'Competing Strategies for Analyzing the Contexts of Social Interaction', *Sociological Inquiry*, 64 (2): 179–98.

Simeoni, Daniel and Marco Diani (eds) (1995) *Current Sociology*, 43 (2/3), Special number on 'Biographical Research'.

Sorenson, Aage (1994) 'Women, Family and Class', *Annual Review of Sociology*, 18: 39–61.

Sorokin, P.A. (1959) *Social and Cultural Mobility*. London: Collier-Macmillan (first published as *Social Mobility* in 1927).

Stanley, Liz and Wise, Sue (1993) *Breaking Out Again: Feminist ontology and epistemology*. 2nd edn. London: Routledge.

Strauss, Anselm and Corbin, Juliet (1998) *Basics of Qualitative Research*. 2nd edn. Thousand Oaks, CA: Sage.

Strauss, W. and Howe, N. (1991) *Generations*. New York, NY: McGraw-Hill.

Thomas, W.I. and Znaniecki, F. (1958) *The Polish Peasant in Europe and America*. New York: Dover Publications (original editions published 1918–1920).

Thompson, Paul (1988) *The Voice of the Past*. 2nd edn. Oxford: Oxford University Press.

Thompson, Paul (1993) 'Family Myth, Models, and Denials in the Shaping of Individual Life Paths', in D. Bertaux and P. Thompson (eds), *Between Generations: Family models, myths, and memories*. Vol. 2, *International Yearbook of Oral History and Life Stories*. Oxford: Oxford University Press. 13–38.

Thompson, P. (1997) 'Women, Men, and Transgenerational Family Influences in Social Mobility', in D. Bertaux and P. Thompson (eds), *Pathways to Social Class: A qualitative approach to social mobility*. Oxford: Clarendon Press.

Tilly, C. (1978) 'Migration in Modern European History', in W.H. McNeill and R.S. Adams (eds), *Human Migration: Patterns and policies*. London: Indiana University Press. 48–72.

Tilly, C. (1992) *History and Sociological Imagining* (Working Paper Series No. 134). New York: New School for Social Research.

Tölke, A. (1987) 'Historische Ausgangssituation und Veränerungen im Ausbildungs-und Erwerbsverhalten junger Frauen in der Nach-kriegszeit', in W. Voges (ed.), *Methoden der Biographie–und Lebens-laufforschung*. Opladen: Leske & Budrich. 389–411.

United States Bureau of the Census (1957) *Statistical Abstract of the United States*. 78th edn. Washington, D.C.: U.S. Bureau of the Census.

United States Bureau of the Census (1983) *Statistical Abstract of the United States*. 103rd edn. Washington, D.C.: U.S. Bureau of the Census.

United States Bureau of the Census (1996) *Statistical Abstract of the United States*. 116th edn. Washington, D.C.: U.S. Bureau of the Census.

Whyte, William Foote (1955) *Street Corner Society.* 2nd edn. Chicago: University of Chicago Press. (1st edn. 1943).

Wilton, Janis (1998) 'Share and Compare: Ideas for teaching oral history' Appendix A, in A. Thomson, *Undergraduate Life History Research Projects: Approaches, issues and outcomes*. Brighton: Centre for Continuing Education, University of Sussex. 25–8.

Index

Page numbers in italics refer to tables and figures.